What is this ?

Ancient questions for modern minds

What a delightful retreat! These Sŏn – Korean Zen – teachings, leavened with contemporary insights and years of study and practice, provide the reader with practical and moving guidance for meditation, and for life itself. Stephen and Martine offer us a warm and caring teaching with underlying rigour and the gift of wisdom. Highly recommended for all of us, and a joy to read!

> – **Pat Enkyo O'Hara**, author of *Most intimate: a Zen approach to life's challenges*

A wonderfully enlightening book about contemporary Sŏn meditation, you will have a first-hand experience of what it is like to sit on a meditation cushion and do the retreat with two highly experienced teachers. I highly recommend it for both seasoned practitioners and newbies.

> – **Haemin Sunim**, author of *The things you can only see when you slow down* and *Love for imperfect things*

This marvellously readable little book will tell you all you need to know about meditation. A transcription of talks from a Sŏn (Korean Zen) retreat, it focuses mainly on the practice of questioning – meditation on the question 'What is this?' is a key practice in Sŏn. Stephen and Martine's lovely words cover the entire ground of meditation practice and its applications to living. An elegant and down-to-earth book by two of our best western Buddhist teachers.

> – **Norman Fischer**, poet, Zen priest, author of *The world could be otherwise: imagination and the Bodhisattva path*

In this practical and inspirational guide to Buddhist practice, Martine and Stephen Batchelor distill a lifetime of personal experience in, and scholarly study of, two distinct types of Buddhist meditation: mindfulness and Zen 'questioning'. Their unique combination of these distinct techniques illustrates how bringing a Zen questioning dimension to mindfulness training can deepen the insight dimension of mindfulness practice and enhance concentration during questioning meditation.

— **Robert E. Buswell,** Jr., University of California, Los Angeles

What an enlightening little book! This book is rich with revelations in how mindfulness can transform the ordinary activities of daily life into the 'everyday sublime'. As Stephen and Martine warmly guide the reader through a Sŏn retreat it comes to life on the page. The practical meditation instructions offer a deep dive of enquiry into the question, 'What is this?', the perennial question that goes to the heart of who we are. The nature of the heart-mind is revealed as they share their personal experience, their in-depth scholarly knowledge, and insights. Martine and Stephen offer a path in how to live a fully engaged life free from reactivity with a heart blown open that embodies integrity, wisdom and compassion.

— **Subhana Barzaghi,** Zen roshi in the Diamond Sangha, guiding teacher for Sydney Zen Centre and Melbourne Zen Group, and senior insight meditation dharma teacher

Also by Martine Batchelor

Buddhism and ecology (1992)

Walking on lotus flowers: Buddhist women living, loving and meditating (1996)

Principles of Zen (1999)

Meditation for life (2001)

Zen (2001)

Women on the Buddhist path (2002)

The path of compassion: the bodhisattva precepts (2004)

Women in Korean Zen: lives and practices (2006)

Let go: a Buddhist guide to breaking free of habits (2007)

The spirit of the Buddha (2010)

Also by Stephen Batchelor

Alone with others: an existential approach to Buddhism (1983)

The Tibet Guide: central and western Tibet (1988)

The faith to doubt: glimpses of Buddhist uncertainty (1990)

The awakening of the west: the encounter of Buddhism and western culture (1994)

Buddhism without beliefs: a contemporary guide to awakening (1997)

Verses from the center: a Buddhist vision of the sublime (2000)

Living with the devil: a meditation on good and evil (2004)

Confession of a Buddhist atheist (2010)

After Buddhism: rethinking the dharma for a secular age (2015)

Secular Buddhism: imagining the dharma in an uncertain world (2017)

The art of solitude (forthcoming)

What is this?

*Ancient questions
for modern minds*

Martine and
Stephen Batchelor

TUWHIRI

Wellington
Aotearoa New Zealand

First edition Gaia House April 2018
Second edition May 2019

Published by
The Tuwhiri Project
PO Box 6626
Wellington 6141
Aotearoa New Zealand
www.tuwhiri.nz

Martine and Stephen Batchelor have generously waived royalty payments for
What is This? All proceeds from the book will go to The Tuwhiri Project.

ISBN 978-0-473-47498-0

A catalogue record for this book is available from the
National Library of New Zealand
Kei te pātengi raraunga o Te Puna Mātauranga o Aotearoa
te whakarārangi o tēnei pukapuka

Design John Houston
Cover photograph by Martine Batchelor
Set in Fira Sans and IBM Plex Serif
Printed by IngramSpark

10 9 8 7 6 5 4 3 2 1

In memory of

Kusan Sunim (1920–1983)
Beop Jeong Sunim (1932–2010)

無 Contents

What is this *Ancient questions for modern minds*

 Preface

What is this? is an edited transcript of the meditation instructions and dharma talks given during a week-long Sŏn Buddhist retreat at Gaia House in Devon, England, from 9–16 April, 2016. Co-led by Stephen and Martine Batchelor, Stephen's opening welcome to the retreatants and concluding remarks before they departed are also included. An abbreviated version of this book was first published by Gaia House in 2018 as part of a fundraising campaign.

'Sŏn' means 'meditation'. It is the Korean equivalent of the Chinese 'Chan' and Japanese 'Zen'. 'Chan' is the way the Chinese pronounced the Pali *jhāna* and Sanskrit *dhyāna*.

What is this? serves as a companion volume to *The faith to doubt: glimpses of Buddhist uncertainty* (1990), most of which Stephen wrote while training as a Sŏn monk in Songgwang Sa monastery, South Korea, from 1981–84. For accounts of the history of Korean Sŏn and life in a Sŏn monastery, as well as the transcripts of their teacher Kusan Sunim's lectures during the winter retreat of 1981–82 at Songgwang Sa, see *The way of Korean Zen* by Kusan Sunim.

We are especially grateful to Jim Champion for transcribing the talks. Without his having done this, the book in your hands would not exist. Jim has also created a series of questions to accompany this book which makes it a useful study tool; you can download them from www.tuwhiri.nz/what-is-this/ together with audio recordings of our talks.

Martine and Stephen Batchelor
Aquitaine, March 2018

What is this? *Ancient questions for modern minds*

Saturday evening

Entering the retreat

Stephen Batchelor

Welcome to Gaia House for the yearly Sŏn retreat. I realise that many of you have travelled a long way to get here, and suspect most of us – like myself – have had a busy week as well. We are all likely to be tired. The mad rush of tying up the loose ends of our lives before setting off for a week of quiet, solitary reflection can be exhausting. We'll keep this opening session short and to the point so everyone can have a good night's sleep.

Martine and I have been leading these retreats once a year since we returned from Songgwang Sa monastery in Korea to Devon in 1985, which would make this retreat the thirtieth – well, actually, the twenty-ninth, since one year we offered this slot to the Chinese Chan master Sheng-yen[1].

First and foremost, this is a retreat: a time of conscious withdrawal from the routines and duties of our everyday existence in order to reflect on what really matters for us. We step back into the solitude and silence offered by Gaia House in order to take stock of ourselves. I imagine many of you will have arrived here with questions or issues that are concerning you. These might have to do with your career, your marriage, your children, or with more personal psychological or spiritual matters. Or it may have to do with the loss of a loved one, a recent diagnosis of sickness, some turning point in your life, or simply your own process of getting older. Or maybe you are here for completely different reasons. It doesn't really matter. What matters is allowing your life to become a question for yourself and being willing to dwell with and deepen that question.

In the old days, coming to Gaia House effectively cut you off from the rest of your life. But with the advent of smartphones, iPads, wifi and the like it is increasingly difficult to do this. Our devices keep us connected with the world no matter where we are. Fortunately, mobile phone reception is very patchy in West Ogwell and we certainly are not going to give you the Gaia House wifi password, so that might help. But the temptation to find a place where you can get a signal and check for or send a text message can be overwhelming at times. I would strongly encourage you to switch your devices off for the duration of this retreat. Or put your tablet on flight mode if you need it to take notes. If you are worried about someone who may need to contact you urgently, then before you go to bed tonight make sure they have the centre's phone number and email address. Then switch your device off. Be assured that the coordinators will let you know as soon as they hear from anyone who needs to contact you.

The silence in which we conduct this retreat is to support the cultivation of a solitude and silence of the mind. We won't be talking except during the discussion periods and interviews with the teachers. If you haven't spent time in silence before, you might at first find this challenging. But with familiarity you will realise that rather than inhibiting communication with others, silence allows us to communicate in a different way. The way we move our bodies, the way we present ourselves through our expression and dress, whether we keep the space around us tidy or messy, small gestures of kindness during the work period or while queuing for meals, glances exchanged when we meet a fellow meditator during a walk in the fields: these are all ways of getting to know each other. I trust that during our days here together we will gradually create a sense of being a temporary sangha, or community.

After a while it may dawn on us that much of what we say to each other in the course of an average day is really not that necessary. Our chatter may be little more than noise to banish the awkwardness of silence. The camaraderie of sharing the joys and hardships of this retreat, of mutually supporting each other's practice in a spirit of generosity, will hopefully become more and more palpable. Although we do not know another person's name or much, if anything, about them, this does not mean we cannot come to cherish their presence. We might also find out at the end of the retreat that all the stories and fantasies we have built up about someone in the room turn out to have had no basis whatsoever. So, be open to one another in a heartfelt way but don't give too much weight to the stories you conjure up around them.

Gaia House is the only place we run a Sŏn retreat. We do it as a way of paying homage to our training in Korea under our teacher Kusan Sunim, as well as of honouring the Imje Sŏn (Rinzai Zen in Japanese) tradition that has developed there. In particular, we are indebted to the work of the twelfth century monk Chinul, who not only founded Songgwang Sa monastery but is one of the key figures in the founding of the Korean Sŏn tradition[2].

Those of you who have been here at Gaia House on other retreats will notice that the room is laid out differently than usual. Like in Sŏn monasteries in Korea, we will be sitting and walking inside the hall. So we have placed you in four rows, divided into two blocks. Those on the outer rows of the two blocks will sit looking at the wall, while those on the inside rows will be looking at the centre of the room facing the others in the opposite row. We will sit in sessions of between thirty to forty minutes, then stand up and walk anticlockwise around the two blocks of cushions for ten or so minutes. If you haven't done this before, it might sound a bit confusing, but you will soon get the hang of it.

Rather than a nice sonorous bell, the periods of sitting and walking will be marked by this wooden clapper called a *djukpi*. We're not going to hit you with it. It's just a piece of bamboo split down the middle that when struck on the palm makes a sharp cracking sound like this: *klak! klak! klak!* It will serve to mark the beginning and end of all practice periods.

The *djukpi* is also used for the morning and evening ceremony when we offer three bows to the Buddha. Again, this reflects how things are done in Korean Sŏn halls. Before the first sit in both the morning and evening, we will offer a bowl of water, a stick of incense and a candle to the Buddha, then bow three times as the *djukpi* strikes. We are not bowing to the Buddha statue behind me as though it were some sacred object, but simply affirming a commitment to what that image stands for: the condition of being awake, which each person, Buddhist or not, is capable of aspiring to and experiencing. I know this sort of thing might seem incongruous if you have come here expecting a secular Buddhist approach, but – hey – we can't always be consistent. If you have any religious or other objections to doing this, then please do not participate.

We will also be conducting fifteen-minute personal interviews every afternoon. With the number we have on this retreat, this means that each person will only have one formal interview. Your turn will follow the order in which you are seated in the two blocks of cushions. Those in the two rows on my side of the hall will see me, and those in the two rows on Martine's side will see her. This will be an opportunity to discuss anything that has come up in your meditation or other questions related to your practice that you would like to explore in private. The interviews will take place in the library, which is just before you get to the circular staircase on the ground floor. If you need to see either of us at any other time, just leave a note on the board or come up to us at the end of the practice sessions. We are here for you. Don't hesitate if you need to talk to either of us about anything.

As a way of kicking this retreat off, I'd like to offer some words of the eighth century Chinese teacher Mazu Daoyi. He said:

> *All of you should realise that your own mind is Buddha, that is, this mind is Buddha's mind. Those who seek for the truth should realise that there is nothing to seek. There is no Buddha but mind; there is no mind but Buddha.*[3]

Mazu's point is very simple. He is saying that whatever we seek to achieve in meditation is already right here before our very eyes. As soon as we use words like 'Buddha' or 'enlightenment' or 'truth' we tend to imagine something that is far away from the condition in which we find ourselves now. Mazu, however, tells us that these things are only ever experienced in the very midst of what it means to be human in this moment. There is no other realm or place where they are to be found. Nor is he saying that they are hidden somewhere in the unconscious depths of our psyche, or in some hitherto undiscovered dimension of consciousness. No, they are right here in the messiness, confusion, darkness and anxiety of the very mind that is listening to these words. And, one could add, the body of the Buddha is nothing but the very body that is sitting on the cushion, its heart beating, its lungs drawing and exhaling each breath, its knees aching from sitting cross-legged. I urge you to stop making a difference between who you think you are and who you think the Buddha is.

Mazu was once asked: 'What is the meaning of Buddhism?' He retorted with another question: 'What is the meaning of this moment?'[4] As we go into this retreat together, it would be a good idea to drop every single notion you have formed about the Buddha and Buddhism. Get rid of any thought you might have of enlightenment. Instead, just sit still in this room, pay attention to what you experience here and now, and let yourself be drawn into the mystery of simply being human, the puzzle of being here at all.

Sunday morning

The basis of meditation

Martine Batchelor

Today I want to look at the basics of meditation. We're embarking on a Sŏn-style retreat in which we pose the question, 'What is this?' I would like to start with this observation: in Buddhist traditions, meditation practice is based on two fundamental elements – *anchoring* and *experiential inquiry*.

The various Buddhist traditions approach these elements in different ways. For example, in the *vipassanā* tradition, the anchor can be the breath or the body. In the Tibetan tradition, you might use a mantra, a visualisation, or a theme. If you look at Japanese Rinzai Zen and Soto Zen, bear in mind that they come from the Chan tradition in China, where two currents predominated: the Lin-Chi/Rinzai current, which uses koans or questions as focuses;

and the Tsao-Tung current – later known as Soto in Japan. Soto Zen taught 'just sitting', a meditation practice also called 'silent illumination'. In the Korean Sŏn tradition, the anchor is a question like: 'What is this?'.

There are different ways to anchor. We can focus on something in the moment, as in the vipassanā tradition, or settle on a question as in the Korean Sŏn tradition. We can also cultivate experiential enquiry in different ways. Vipassanā practitioners, for example, do it by being aware of change. In the Korean Sŏn tradition, we focus on questioning and experiential inquiry. In any tradition, anchoring and inquiry are developed together to become creative awareness or creative mindfulness. We might practise them in different ways, but these two aspects remain the essential components of the practice. So when we're sitting in meditation, we're basically cultivating these two elements together.

Rather than use the term 'concentration', I'd prefer to use the word 'anchoring', because we have an unhelpful relationship to 'concentration'. If somebody tells us, 'Concentrate!', generally we tense up and try to narrow our focus. Anchoring is a better image, because it brings to mind anchoring a boat. We have the anchor, we have the boat, and thanks to the anchor the boat is not going to drift away. The boat isn't stationary – it shifts a little according to the current and wind – but it's not going very far.

So we see that the anchor – the breath, the body, sound, or a question – actually helps us to be with our experience. As Stephen said, the aim is to be with our life in this moment, in an open and stable way. In the Sŏn tradition, we come back to the question, 'What is this?'. The crucial aspect of anchoring – whether we're coming back to the breath, or coming back to the question 'What is this?' – is that we come back to the whole experience of this moment.

When we're sitting here with nothing to do but cultivate

meditation – anchoring and questioning – we might notice that a lot of the time we're somewhere else. Just as we can't stop ourselves hearing, we can't stop ourselves thinking. Rather, we're creating space so we're not *too* lost in thoughts. What we might notice as we sit is that, yes, we're going to have thoughts, and a lot of the time the thoughts are going to be fairly repetitive. Maybe from time to time, we'll have a new thought, and sometimes we might think creative thoughts, but most of the time it's repetitive. It's the same with sounds. As we go through the day sounds repeat: the sounds of birds, the sounds of cars, the sounds outside. It's the same with sensations in the body: some will come again and again.

Repetition is part of life, but we don't want to become stuck in it. From time to time, we have thoughts we've never had before, just as from time to time we hear sounds we've never heard before. As we anchor, the point is not to stop the functioning of the organism. We think, we see, we hear, we taste, we smell, we experience sensations, we have thoughts. This is just the organism functioning. Anchoring helps us to open up some space, so it's not so relentless – not so repetitive and automatic. Thus we can experience some freedom, some creativity and spaciousness. We can exercise choice. Do I want to continue to think these thoughts? Do I want to continue to be with these sensations?

When we focus on inquiry, our anchoring consists in returning again and again to the question, and to notice that when we're lost in thoughts, we're not totally here with this multi-perspectival experience. Rather, we're caught in just one aspect of it, which often references the past or the future. In returning to the question we train ourselves to be here, bringing creative awareness – creative *engagement* – to this moment. And we can only do this by accessing our experience in each moment.

It is very important to see that when we anchor – when we focus – we don't hold onto the breath for dear life. Nor do we hold onto the question tensely. Instead, we use them as an anchor in our experience. We come back to them again and again, and cultivate choice: do I continue with this, or do I return to the question? That's the choice we have: we can continue with a certain thought, or come back to our whole experience via the anchor.

When we come back to the question or to the breath, four things are going to happen. Firstly, we're not going to feed the repetition. Secondly, we weaken the power of the repetition. Thirdly, we bring our attention back to the whole moment. And finally, we bring ourself back to our creative functioning, which to me is an important part of the practice. This can help us become calmer, more spacious and stable.

The other aspect of the practice, which is just as important, is experiential inquiry. We can be aware of change – sounds, breath, changing sensations – or we can just ask the question: 'What is this?'. In this way we question our tendency to fixate, to identify: 'I am like this', or 'This is like that'. And by cultivating questioning – asking 'What is this?' – we generate more openness. We learn to be with uncertainty, which sensitises us to change. Thus we can experience change through questioning, or we can experience change through looking directly at change.

We can cultivate mindfulness either directly or indirectly, just as we can cultivate awareness of change directly or indirectly. I realised this as a nun in Korea where, for ten years, I just practised asking the question 'What is this?' in meditation, and nothing else. Through doing this I quickly became more aware, more compassionate, and more conscious of change. In this way I became more alert to conditions.

What works best for you is the important thing. Does it make more sense to cultivate mindfulness and awareness of change directly? Or do you use a method such as returning to the question 'What is this?'? You will still be cultivating awareness of change, but in another way. For someone who is used to Sŏn practice this will be obvious, while others may want to see how they can bring these two approaches together.

Personally, I undertook the Sŏn questioning first, then explored awareness practice, and I find they complement each other very well. This is an issue we can explore together during this week. For those not familiar with questioning, I will now introduce the method, and Stephen will talk more about its history later.

If we're using the question when we're sitting, we just ask (inwardly, silently), 'What is this?'. But we need to note that this practice is about questioning; it's not a practice of answering. The Japanese Zen tradition developed something else later; but within the Sŏn tradition we're trying to cultivate a sensation of questioning in the whole body and mind. The anchor is the question, and we come back to the question again and again. You'll notice that if you come back to the question, you come back to the whole experience of the moment.

The other aspect of the practice is experiential enquiry, which means we're not repeating the question like a mantra. We're not sitting there silently chanting *What-is-this?-What-is-this?-What-is-this?* The most important part of the question is the question mark itself. You might say, 'But what is this?'. You might think that this question is a little vague, and wonder what, precisely, you're asking about. We're not asking about anything in particular. When you ask 'What is this?' you're throwing the question into the moment, which gives you direct access to being in the moment. We ask 'What is this?' not as a way to define the experience of the moment, nor to fix it, but just as a way to open to it. So it's important to see that the aim is to open to the moment without defining anything.

If you're used to practising vipassanā or mindfulness meditation, you can use it in what I would call a modern way. You might be sitting there, then a thought arises, and you might ask 'What is this?' to gain a different relationship to it. Traditionally, we just ask the question with no reference points, it's a totally open-ended question. At this level it's not an analysis; we're not engaging in psychological or philosophical research. We're not delving into the meaning of the universe! Rather, we're deploying a method whereby we can cultivate anchoring and inquiry together.

Crucially, *we're trying to balance the elements of calmness and brightness.* I will talk more about this aspect later. If you're used to meditating on the breath, and if you think the question is attracting lots of thoughts or is agitating you, you can always come back to the breath or the body – something that is calming. If you feel a little sleepy, and you're used to watching the breath which can be calming and a little sleep-inducing, then ask the question 'What is this?'. It could help to wake you up.

There are many different ways to put the question. I recommend two main ways. First up, we can synchronise it with the breath, as one teacher in Korea presented it. You breathe in, and as you breathe out you ask, 'What is this?'. You breathe in, and as you breathe out you ask, 'What is this?' again. Try that a little, if you like. But be careful not to let the practice lead you into controlling the breath in any way. This is not a yoga exercise. You let the breath come in, and when it naturally leaves the body you ask the question.

Alternatively you can ask the question and stay with the sensation of questioning – the unknowing – while it's there; and when that sensation subsides, you can go back to the silent wording of the question 'What is this?'. Above all, don't ask the question with the head. You really don't want to do this because it'll give you a headache! Draw the question down and ask it from the belly. Ask it from a feeling of the belly: 'What is this?'. Try to pose it with the whole body and mind, without tensing around it. This is important, because sometimes when we meditate we try to focus or question with the body in a tense way. Or we might try to force it with the body, scrunching the head for example. In our practice here we sit in a relaxed, upright posture, and then try to bring the question down to the belly: 'What is this?'.

Like any method, this one might not work for everybody. During the week, try to see what is more helpful for you, because we'll also talk about the breath, and about sounds.

Some people really take to this practice, and that's fine. But some people may find themselves sitting there asking, 'What is this... what is that... why am I asking this stupid question?'. If that's the way you feel, don't persist with this approach. No method is sacred. The breath, the body, sound, loving kindness, just sitting, questioning – they're all just tools, techniques, so just try it out lightly, with no obligation. Does it work, or not? Can you combine it with something else, or not? This is for you to see.

Some people focus on the question and it seems to pro-voke thoughts. If that happens, try reverting to mindfulness of the breath, mindfulness of the body, mindfulness of sound, and just from time to time – maybe once or twice in a thirty minute medi-tation session – you can drop in the question. But not too much if it has a thought-generating effect.

Some people feel a little anxious when they ask the ques-tion. If that's what happens for you, go back to mindfulness of the breath, body or sound, and from time to time introduce the ques-tion. We're trying to cultivate quietness and clarity together. So see which element can help you here. Questioning can definitely help us with clarity, and for some people it's a very good anchoring element. Others might choose to use the body or the breath as an anchoring element.

Then you can play a little with what I call the foreground

and the background. Remember, the question opens up a broad and deep focus. We're not asking 'What is this? What is this?' to shut everything out – that's not the idea! Rather, we're asking 'What is this?' in the *foreground*, while in the *background* we have a wide open awareness, where we have thoughts, sensations, hear sounds, and notice feelings that arise and pass away. So put the question in the foreground, and everything else in the background. At times, though, you could have sound in the foreground, or the breath, possibly with the question in the background, or no question at all. Then introduce it again from time to time, and see how it works.

Sometimes you might have the question in the foreground, then a bit of sound in the background, then everything else. See how it works with foreground and background. Sometimes something might move to the foreground, at which point what was at first in the foreground will now move to the background. This is early in our week together, so we want to try things out.

Another factor is posture. As this is a Sŏn practice there'll be a lot of sitting, like Chan style – Bodhidharma style. We're going to sit for thirty minutes and then walk in the room for ten minutes, so when we sit on the first day we're trying the practice out. If you sit on the floor, try with a cushion or a bench. Ask yourself: do I need a cushion under my knees? Do I need to be a little bit higher so I can tilt forward a little more? Is it better to sit on a bench? If you sit on a bench you might have less back problems, but more knee problems. So choose which to go for, experiment a little. If after sitting for five minutes you're in agony, try sitting on a chair. But if you sit for twenty minutes and only then, towards the end of the sit, it's a little uncomfortable, you know that in ten minutes you're going to walk. At that point it's okay to persist. If the discomfort subsides after you've been standing and walking for two minutes, then go back to your posture. But if the pain continues through the day, consider sitting on a chair, or find a different posture.

If you sit on a chair, I would recommend sitting in the middle of the chair the way I do so that you can hold your back upright yourself. But if you have pain in the back and you need to sit at the back of the chair, I'd recommend finding a way to still sit relatively straight-backed, perhaps with a cushion or a folded blanket between the back of the chair and your back. This way you won't slouch, which in turn will make it easier for you to remain alert.

Sunday evening

TALK

Questioning and responding

Stephen Batchelor

I'm going to start with where we find ourselves at this moment. And since I don't know how you find yourselves, I'm afraid I will have to talk about myself.

What I'm experiencing right now is that thing I encounter each time I sit down on a cushion and pay attention to what is happening. Yet every time I find myself utterly incapable of putting whatever it is I'm experiencing into words. There's something about the practice of meditation, whether it be Sŏn or any exercise where we are asked just to pay attention to what is happening, in which we find ourselves confronted with what philosophers call the sheer facticity of our existence.

This is the inescapable fact of being this being that I am.

When I look inside, or say to myself, 'I'm looking inside' – whatever that might mean, I seem to hit up against something that is intimately present to me, but impossible to define. It always strikes me in the first instance as a particular sensation in the body, in the chest or stomach somewhere. It depends. I was reminded a few days ago of a passage by William James who said:

> *...it may be truly said that the 'self of selves', when carefully examined, is found to consist mainly of the collection of these peculiar motions in the head or between the head and throat... it would follow that our entire feeling of spiritual activity, or what commonly passes by that name, is really a feeling of bodily activities whose exact nature is by most men overlooked.*[5]

Anyone who has spent time doing such introspection, whether in meditation or just out of curiosity about who you are, can probably recognise what James was on about. It's curious that in pursuing such 'deep' questions about the nature of who I am, in the end, if I'm utterly honest with myself, what presents itself is a completely banal physical sensation.

Some years ago in the 1990s I spent a couple of days in Nagi Gompa, a nunnery up in the hills above Kathmandu in Nepal, where I went to study Dzogchen with a teacher called Urgyen Tulku.[6] From him I received what is called the 'pointing out instruction' in which one is initiated, as it were, into the practice of Dzogchen.

This instruction entails listening to a direct presentation from the teacher who points out to you the nature of your mind, or – even more than that – the nature of what they call rigpa, a primordial, pristine awareness that is more than your ordinary, everyday mind. But the problem was that no matter how much Urgyen Tulku tried to point this out to me, what I found myself actually aware of was a physical sensation somewhere in my body.

Of course, when I told him this, he said 'No! Look! It is without form, without shape, without colour, without sensation', and so on. But however much I was told what *rigpa* was, I could not get beyond a physical sensation somewhere in my body. Before I could think of mind or consciousness or awareness I felt this strange, indefinable sensation – like William James' funny sensations in the back of the throat. I wasn't cut out to be a Dzogchen practitioner. I experience exactly the same thing when doing mindfulness or any meditative practice that supposedly brings one into a greater understanding of one's mind or mental states. In my Sŏn training in Korea, my teacher Kusan Sunim was very keen on what he called *shin* (or *maum* in colloquial Korean), which is the Chinese-Korean-Japanese word for the Pali word *citta* – 'mind', or 'heart-mind' if you wish, but in his teaching it was really not very different from the rigpa of Dzogchen. When Kusan Sunim taught us to ask 'What is this?' for him the 'this' meant shin.

He made it very clear that shin was not our ordinary, every-day consciousness or awareness. Shin, like rigpa, was somehow far more. It lay behind the scenes, hidden from view, and the purpose of meditative enquiry was to break through to it, to experience it directly. And such would be – in my teacher's understanding – the experience of enlightenment. But from the beginning of my training I found myself highly sceptical of this language. I was resistant to the idea of there being 'something more', something beyond what we can see-hear-smell-taste-touch and know with our ordinary mind.

There is a tension in the Sŏn tradition between an emphasis on the everyday specificity of experience – all the talk about cypress trees in the courtyard, pounds of flax and so on, and a rather mystical teaching about a transcendent or universal mind or consciousness – similar to what you might find in Advaita Vedanta: the notion of some non-dual awareness. As much as I've tried to figure out what my teacher meant by shin, I'm still just as confused about it as I was on day one. I'm not at all persuaded that it is a useful way of presenting this practice.

By 'this practice' I don't just mean the particular meditation we're doing on this retreat, but 'practice' in the wider sense of trying to be fully human, to lead a life in which I'm completely honest with myself. A practice in which I'm cautious about taking on trust claims about the nature of some transcendent awareness or reality that I consistently fail to have any immediate sense of in my life.

What often creeps into Buddhism, including Sŏn, is the notion that there is something more than this experience that we're having right now, that we need to break through into this something else. It's a very seductive idea that's characteristic of most traditions that would consider themselves to be 'mystical'. Whether they speak in terms of 'God', 'the Absolute' or 'the Unconditioned', there's often an underlying assumption that what we're experiencing now is somehow not enough, it's inadequate, at best only a tiny bit of something far vaster. And the practices that are taught in these traditions provide us with a methodology, which if we follow enables us to reach this 'something else'.

I'm reminded here of a short *sutta*, a discourse, in the *Connected discourses of the Buddha*, which is called the *Sabba sutta*. *Sabba* means 'everything' or 'the all'. Gotama says:

> *Mendicants, I will teach you the all. Listen to this. And what is the all? The eye and forms, the ear and sounds, the nose and odours, the tongue and tastes, the body and tactile sensations, the mind and dharmas. This is called the all. If anyone, mendicants, should speak thus: 'Having rejected this all, I shall make known another all' – that would be a mere empty boast on his part. If he were questioned he would not be able to reply and,*

further, he would meet with vexation. For what reason? Because, monks, that all would not be within his domain.[7]

Now I find this passage terribly engaging. You find a similar approach in the writings of Nāgārjuna and Madhyamaka philosophy, where there's also a deep suspicion of the idea that the purpose of practice is to lead us to something outside of what we can see, hear, smell, taste, touch and know within our own moment-to-moment, ordinary consciousness. And it's this, I feel, that characterises the early Sŏn tradition. My sense is that Sŏn started life in China as an explicit rejection of a grandiose mysticism that had begun seeping into Buddhism. The early Sŏn masters had no time at all for notions of an 'Ultimate Truth' that lies beyond our ordinary experience. Instead, it sought to recover the simplicity and the primacy of the experience we're having in this body, in these senses, in this flesh, right now. That's where we begin.

The legend of the Buddha himself points to the same thing. It was by waking up to the existential facts of his own life that prompted him to embark on his quest. The fact of birth, the fact of sickness, the fact of ageing and the fact of death became questions for him. These experiences are utterly of this breathing, feeling body. And that's where we begin too. That's what we come back to, again and again and again when our minds wander off into the past, into the future, or simply into unstructured threads of associated thought. We come back to the dull, blunt immediacy that is intimate but inarticulate: in other words, what we are experiencing right now.

When I ask myself the question 'What is this?', by 'this' I don't mean some sort of mystical citta, or shin, or rigpa. By 'this' I mean the totality of what you're experiencing in this moment right now. Whatever that might be.

To try and understand better what Kusan Sunim meant by

shin as the object of 'What is this?', I went back to the Ming edition of the Chinese text of the *Platform sutra* where the account of the story behind 'What is this?' is found. What I discovered was that the text makes no mention at all of *shin* or mind. It simply speaks of this 'thing' – *bulgon*, in Korean. The question 'What is this?' is presented as 'What is this *thing*?' I like the word 'thing'. 'Thing' has a kind of gritty immediacy to it. It's one of those words we use all the time, but rarely stop to consider what it means. What is a *thing*? It's a terribly difficult question, just as hard to answer as 'What is consciousness?', or 'What is the mind?'.

So what is a thing? What is *this* thing? What is this thing in all of its stripped-bare vulnerability, ineffability, banality? What is that? What is this thing that was thrust into the world at birth? This thing that will get sick, that will get old, that will die. What is it?

As far as possible, let go of any ideas about this that you may have acquired, whether they be Buddhist or Sŏn doctrines or other theories or beliefs you may have picked up from different religious or philosophical traditions. Just try to put all of that stuff out of your mind. Particularly transcendent or mystical ideas to which you might have become attached.

After three or four years of training in Tibetan Buddhism in India, I had one of those experiences that come upon you out of the blue. I was walking through the woods above McLeod Ganj lugging a bucket of water that I'd just got from the nearby standpipe and all of a sudden found myself just stopped in my tracks and simply overwhelmed by the utter strangeness of what was happening. The incredible weirdness of just being there, of standing in that forest with a bucket of water hanging from my right arm. This was an experience that has informed pretty much everything else I've done in my practice, my writing work and my teaching since. It struck me very strongly then – long before I knew anything much about Sŏn – that this must be the primary questioning and wonder that give rise to philosophy or religion in the first place. If we are open to it, we realise that life itself in its gritty simplicity is profoundly and overwhelmingly mysterious.

Yet as creatures who have been designed by biology and evolution to survive, we're not, I think, really prepared to experience things this way. I suspect such moments as the one I described are an unintended consequence of having evolved brains sufficiently complex for the emergence of language and self-reflexive awareness to emerge. Unlike all other animals, we are conscious of the fact that we will die. As a byproduct of a consciousness that may have evolved for entirely different reasons, we have acquired the capacity to become questions for ourselves.

And this practice of Sŏn – in fact the practice of the dharma, period – is a practice of coming to terms with the question of who and what we are. This requires that we allow ourselves to be a mystery for ourselves rather than a set of more or less interesting facts. I suspect most human beings at certain moments in their lives experience something similar. It might come about through being in nature, through art, through falling in love, through studying philosophy, or when coming close to death. Any moment when suddenly we are overwhelmed by the fact that we are here at all, rather than not here.

In the western tradition, this way of thinking goes back at least to Socrates, who said that 'wonder is the beginning of philosophy'. Leibnitz, and then later Heidegger, ponder the question 'Why is there anything at all, rather than just nothing?'. That question has always functioned for me as a *kongan*, or *kōan* in Japanese. It may not have the same effect for everyone, but when I first read this question, it sent a shiver up my spine. This is very similar, I think, to what in Sŏn is called 'cultivating the sensation of doubt'. There's something physical about it, something that reverberates through one's body. We're not talking here of a purely mental or spiritual experience. We're talking of something that is palpably somatic.

In the kongan collection called *The gateless gate*, the compiler Wumen Huikai says that you must question with your entire body 'making the 360 bones and joints and 84,000 pores into a solid lump of doubt'.[8] Now, of course, that's not meant literally, but we probably all know what he means. It's that kind of questioning that goes beyond just an intellectual curiosity or puzzlement and has become a vital, embodied perplexity in which we can no longer meaningfully distinguish between body and mind. It feels as though the whole of us, every cell of our body, is seized with this sense of doubt.

What I also like about the early teachings of the Sŏn tradition is their repeated emphasis on the specific details of ordinary life. You are probably familiar with some of these kongans:

> *'Why did Bodhidharma come from the west?'*
> *Zhaozhou answers: 'The cypress tree in the courtyard.'*[9]

> *'What is the Buddha?'*
> *Dongshan said: 'Three pounds of flax.'*[10]

> *'What is the teaching that goes beyond everything the Buddhas and the Patriarchs ever said?'*
> *To which Yunmen replies: 'Cake.'*[11]

You completely miss the point if you think that these are answers to those questions. They're not. They're shock tactics, ways of jolting the student's attention away from those kinds of questions altogether and bringing it back to what is right before her eyes, to whatever is visibly, tangibly present at the moment she asked the question.

'The cypress tree in the courtyard.' I can only imagine that this took place in a room, outside of which there stood a cypress tree. By getting drawn into speculative questions about Bodhidharma's motives for coming to China from India, which could no doubt lead to some fascinating discussions, we are taken away, in increasingly rarefied steps of abstraction, from the actual situation at hand so that we don't even see the cypress tree in the courtyard any more. We've gone off into the land of metaphysics and doctrine and theory. Terribly interesting, but we've lost sight of the tree.

As for the business of the three pounds of flax, I imagine the monks sorting through the flax that they had harvested that day in the monastery's fields. One of them asks the teacher Dongshan a question about the Buddha. But the teacher abruptly turns the monks' attention away from such theorising and back to what they're doing there and then. They're sorting flax.

And I imagine Yunmen sitting on a chair or platform, with a low table in front of him. As is often the case in those monasteries, there would be a cup of tea, a plate of cakes – in this case probably pounded rice cakes of some kind. But rather than get drawn into the question that's being asked about some special, esoteric teaching, Yunmen turns the monk's attention to a lump of rice cake.

I think all these stories – of which there are many – are basically doing the same thing. They cut through a particular habit of the human mind. As soon as the student gets drawn into questions about truth, the meaning of life, philosophy and religion, the teacher bluntly and abruptly severs the tendency to speculate and points to the immediacy of what's actually at hand. For what is at hand is what is truly mysterious and worthy of questioning: a piece of cake, a pile of flax, a cypress tree.

We see this in early Buddhism too, in the Pali texts. I think something similar is going on. Yet in Indian tradition there's a general tendency – why, I don't know – to avoid referring to specific objects in the world, like a piece of cake, a pile of flax, or a particular tree. Instead, the emphasis tends to be placed more on subjective states of consciousness. Yet when the Buddha speaks of meditation in the early texts – let's say the *Satipaṭṭhāna sutta*, the discourse on the establishing of mindfulness – he does not instruct his monks and followers to meditate on the nature of mind, the experience of emptiness, or anything abstract and transcendent like God. Instead he says: go into a forest, sit cross-legged at the foot of a tree, and when you know you're breathing in you know that you're breathing in, and when you know you're breathing out you know that you're breathing out.[12]

Now in the context of Indian religious and philosophical thought that is a very shocking thing to say. It goes completely against the stream of metaphysical thinking that is so characteristic of Indian religion and philosophy, which emphasise realisation of Brahman – God, and *ātman* – the true self. In order to experience such transcendent things one is instructed to disassociate oneself from the physical and phenomenal world. Then this teacher comes along and says: 'No! Just sit down at the foot of a tree and when you breathe in know that you're breathing in, and when you breathe out know that you're breathing out.' Again, as in Sŏn, it's a shock tactic that brings us back to what is immediately at hand.

This is further expanded in the *Satipaṭṭhāna sutta* by telling the meditator to then contemplate all the different parts of the body. The hair on the head. The brain. The eyes. The skin. The flesh. The mucus. The lymph. The urine. The faeces, and so on. Sometimes these reflections are explained as a way of putting the monks and nuns off sex or having sexual fantasies, but I think that's missing the point. It's about coming back to the sheer facticity of our physical existence, in its most basic and irreducible sense. Our guts. Our shit. Our skin. Our sweat. Our blood. That's where we focus attention.

And only from there do we go into feelings, but again, feelings that are triggered by our encounters with the physical world. Perceptions, the way that we make sense of that. Impulses, and so on. Until we arrive at what Gotama simply calls *sabbe dhamma* – all things. And all things are, as we've seen, what we see, hear, smell, taste, touch, feel. For many 'spiritual' people this is deeply counterintuitive: to turn attention away from mystical truths back to the brute simplicity of where we are in our bodies, in this moment, right now.

Nowhere is this more beautifully expressed than in the Epicurean poem *The nature of things* by the Roman poet Lucretius. This is how it appears in A.E. Stallings' translation:

> *Behold the pure blue of heavens, and all that they possess,*
> *The roving stars, the moon, the sun's light, brilliant and sublime*
> *–*
>
> *Imagine if these were shown to men now for the first time,*
> *Suddenly and with no warning. What could be declared*
> *More wondrous than these miracles no one before had dared*
> *Believe could even exist? Nothing. Nothing could be quite*
> *As remarkable as this, so wonderful would be the sight.*
> *Now, however, people hardly bother to lift their eyes*
> *To the glittering heavens, they are so accustomed to the skies.*[13]

Although this Lucretian thought experiment uses the – for us – somewhat clichéd example of the night sky, the poet could just as well have spoken of a cypress tree, a pile of flax or a rice cake. It makes no difference. If you had never seen any such things before and were suddenly shown them, it would have the same shock effect as seeing the night sky for the first time.

This is what the Sŏn tradition does – particularly the early tradition, before Sŏn too got caught up in ideas about shin, Universal Mind, and so on. It was all about recovering the primary experience that we are encountering in this very moment right now. All of us. The stuff that feels somehow dull, inert, maybe a bit boring, overly familiar. But that's where we begin, and – I would argue – that's also where we end. Except we end up discovering how what we look upon as ordinary is, in fact, utterly extraordinary. There's nothing I can think of that is stranger than just being here now. Nothing more mysterious, nothing more transcendent. The problem is that we have got stuck into a habit of thinking that denigrates ordinary life as somehow inferior, somehow just a pale shadow of reality.

This goes back all the way to Plato, of course. In Plato's parable of the cave people find themselves in a dark cavern, and there is just a little fire burning that throws shadows onto the walls, and people think that that's the nature of reality. 'But no!' some smart person says, 'You can get out of this cave! And then you will get to another realm altogether, with brilliant sunlight and colours. What you see in this cave is at best just a very poor copy.' This kind of idealism, I think, has characterised so much of our western tradition in philosophy and theology – the idea that there's a more true world somewhere else, but not here.

The parable of Plato's cave reinforces the very habit that Gotama and Sŏn seek to overcome. It serves to diminish this world in which we actually live. We don't live in Plato's cave, we live in this world, which is not a pale copy of some truer reality. Yet both in India and the west, our traditions of thought have often rendered it as such.

If we could just learn to pay attention to the ordinary things: our breath, our footsteps, the trees around us, the sounds of the rooks in the trees. If we could attend to this mundane world in a different way, in a way in which we attend to it with a greater stillness and clarity of mind – not a mind that's constantly trying to figure out what's going on through the veil of mental chatter and habit – if we could quieten that chatter. And at the same time if we could open our hearts and our minds to just notice what we see, what we hear, what we smell, what we taste, what we touch, how we feel. And this, of course, is the practice of mindfulness.

Sŏn practice injects *curiosity* into mindfulness. This is a term you don't really find in the early Buddhist tradition. You have the idea of *dhamma vicaya*, one of the factors of awakening, which is usually translated as 'analysis of things', but this suggests something rather more cerebral and intellectual. The curiosity or perplexity in Sŏn has nothing much to do with examining things in this way. You hear little about investigating the three marks of being: impermanence, dukkha, and not-self – which is certainly worthwhile – but rather the need to valorise and cultivate an innate astonishment or puzzlement, that sense of how odd things are.

In Korean it's called *ŭisim*, which is usually translated as 'doubt,' but that doesn't quite get it. It's really more like 'perplexity', 'puzzlement', we might even say 'bewilderment' or 'confusion'. There's a well-known verse that Kusan Sunim used to repeat all the time:

> *Great perplexity, great awakening.*
> *Little perplexity, little awakening.*
> *No perplexity, no awakening.*

In other words, the degree to which your practice resonates at a certain pitch of perplexity or doubt, that is the pitch at which your insight or awakening will also resonate.

So if you come to your practice with a mere intellectual curiosity then, as a correlate, any insight that occurs will likewise be intellectual in nature. But let's imagine you come to the practice with a deep existential perplexity – an urgent confusion and puzzlement about what it means to have been born, to get sick, to get old, to die. If that's the pitch at which your practice resonates, then you are allowing the possibility of an insight or an understanding, maybe even a cathartic resolution of that confusion, to emerge at a comparable level of intensity.

Such an insight is unlikely to present itself in doctrinal terms or as a carefully articulated theory. It's far more likely to be expressed as a physical gesture, a line of verse, a spontaneous brush stroke. Sometimes in Sŏn texts you have the monk express his understanding as a shout, a yell – 'HAK!' At least that's how it's transcribed in Korean. In English it might be 'Aha!' or 'Holy shit!'. The trouble is that this quickly gets zenny. These gestures become clichéd and predictable, the exact opposite of the spontaneity they were originally meant to display. There is no point in just aping a kind of language and behaviour.

To my mind, the most compelling and enduring expressions of this kind of insight are found in the visual arts of China, Korea and Japan. I particularly like those of the 18th century Japanese painter Sengai.[14] His works are just ink sketches of a frog, a cat, a snail on a leaf, a bereft old man, a laughing monk, or simply a square, a triangle and a circle, executed with very rapid brushstrokes. Utterly ordinary things. But what Sengai and other Sŏn artists achieve are great works of art. They may just depict frogs, brooms and persimmons, but in such a way that enables you to see these things as if for the first time. With simplicity, economy and spontaneity they do not merely represent these objects but allow them to echo the specific situations in which they belong. It's an aesthetic of poignancy that somehow resonates in our bones. We are moved by it. There's something about the painting that speaks to us at a deep, visceral level and engages our attention. And it brings the mind to a stop. This is true, of course, with great art in all traditions. The arts that come out of Chan or Sŏn or Zen articulate, I think, an understanding that has been prompted not by some deep insight into the nature of ultimate truth, but into having come into a new relationship with the ordinary objects of our daily life.

I very much hope that on this retreat we can practise and learn from some of these examples. And so when we're eating our rice and veggies at lunch, or when we are washing our mug after having had a cup of tea, or during the work period in the garden or the kitchen or the toilets, to incorporate these activities of ordinary life into the practice of Sŏn. These give us a concrete opportunity to deal with the banal objects of the everyday, and yet with the kind of attention that we're seeking to cultivate here, we're given the opportunity to experience them in a completely different light.

To experience ourselves: our breath, the sensations in the body, the pain in the knees, the feeling of the wind or the rain on our cheeks. All of this is utterly pertinent to this question I am suggesting you ask: 'What is this?' But please remember that the 'this' refers to what is so close to you that you tend to completely overlook it.

Monday morning

What is This?

Stephen Batchelor

Today I want to look at the source of the question 'What is this?'. Of course the true source of this question lies within ourselves. It's a question that gives voice to the question of our own existence. And by that I don't just mean my personal existence in this body sitting on this chair, but also everything that made this possible, all the conditions that have given rise over the last fifteen billion or so years to what we are now.

So when you ask yourself 'What is this?', be careful not to narrow the sense of 'this' just to what is palpable within the confines of your own skin. Remember that 'this' also refers to the totality of what is present to you in this moment. One might even say what is prior to the distinction between self and other, you and me, you and the world. Before I think that I am here and you are there. Something primordial, perhaps like the sense of world an unformed child might have.

In Sŏn the source of this question goes back to an encounter between two monks. One is Huineng, the sixth patriarch of Chan in China, that is, after Bodhidharma, who came from south India in the 6th century. Huineng lived in a monastery called Nánhuá Sì which is about a day's journey from Guangzhou in the south of China, not far from Hong Kong. A monastery which, by the way, survived the ravages of the Cultural Revolution and managed to preserve Huineng himself. In the hall of the patriarchs, behind the main temple, you will find Huineng seated inside an ornate glass case. When he died in 713, his body was coated in thick, shiny black lacquer and mummified. I saw this eerie but moving figure when I visited Nánhuá Sì in the mid-eighties after leaving Korea.

The other monk was called Huairang and about Huairang we know very little. But it is with him that this story begins. Huairang lived on Mount Song, which is quite far north in China, near the city of Luoyang. It is supposedly the place where Bodhidharma spent nine years meditating in a cave, staring at the wall. Anyway, Huairang heard of this meditation teacher Huineng and decided to travel south to study with him. So he walked the several hundred miles from Mount Song to Nánhuá Sì. On arriving at the monastery he was ushered in to see the great patriarch.

Huineng said to him: 'Well, where have you come from?' and Huairang replied: 'I've come from Mount Song'. Then Huineng said: 'But what is this thing? How did it get here?' Huairang was speechless. After which, the text tells us, Huairang spent eight years in the monastery.

After eight years – the text doesn't tell us anything about what he did during this time – he goes to see Huineng again. And

Huineng says: 'Okay, what is it?' and Huairang says: 'To say it is like something misses the point'.

End of story.

So the question 'What is this?' or 'What is this thing and how did it get here?' or simply 'What is it?' has its beginnings in this pithy encounter, which I will now try to pick apart.

The story hinges on a conversation, which shifts from a polite exchange of social niceties – 'Oh hello, where have you come from?', 'I've come from Mount Song' – into another kind of discourse altogether when Huineng suddenly asks, 'What is this thing? How did it get here?'.

Huineng is no longer playing the game of social niceties. He's turned the tables, he's changed the rules. He confronts Huairang with the question of his own existence. 'Okay, I know your name, you come from Mount Song, you have this nicely organised story about you and your life, your little personal narrative that you keep running as a monologue in your head. Well, that's all very interesting, but what's actually going on with you?' That's the question. And it's really no different from the question that the young Gotama would have asked himself on seeing an old person, a sick person, a corpse. All of a sudden, these things are no longer just unpleasant features of life but encounters that turn your life around. He has become conscious for the first time of what they call in Chinese 'the great matter of birth and death'.

Huineng turns the conversation from everyday matter-of-fact stuff where we just run on automatic pilot and muddle along, to something more fundamental and shocking. Huairang's speech-lessness is a way of showing that this question threw him back into the primary confusion or perplexity or doubt as to what he was. So urgent had this question become, that he spends the next eight years in the monastery.

I'm very wary about presenting such *kongans* as riddles and the Sŏn teacher as someone whose job it is to help you crack these riddles, so that when you have solved one, you can then go on to solve another one. In Japan this is often how the training proceeds. It is called 'koan study' and requires working through numerous koans over several years. Never having done this training my-self, I am not speaking from experience, so I admit that I might be missing something. But in the Chinese and Korean traditions this is not how kongans are approached. I was always taught that if you resolve one kongan, you resolve all kongans. And the reason for this, which makes a lot of sense, is because all these different kongans – there are supposedly around 1700 of them – are just different ways of posing the same fundamental kongan, which is the kongan of your own existence. In other words, these stories are a means to connect you to the question of the great matter of birth and death. But unlike a riddle, you do not solve the great matter of birth and death and then go on to solve something else. For life is not a riddle. It's a mystery. Coming to terms with, or penetrating into this mystery does not make it any less mysterious. If anything, it makes it *more* mysterious.

Sŏn practice is about opening yourself to this mystery, al-lowing yourself to become totally immersed in the perplexity or wonder it evokes, so that it begins slowly to permeate your con-sciousness as a whole, not just when you're formally sitting in med-itation in this room, but as you go about the everyday business of your life. Whether you're sitting cross-legged on a cushion, peeling potatoes in the kitchen, or getting off the train in Newton Abbot, you start to realise how utterly strange all this is. It takes hold of you more and more and becomes part of your felt-sense of being in the world. Questioning infuses your awareness. Experience may come alive in a startling and puzzling way. And this may be un-comfortable or distressing. But no matter what is happening, one honours the fact of simply being alive in that moment.

This retreat will give us an opportunity over the next week to focus on cultivating this felt-sense of perplexity. Sŏn texts talk of developing a 'mass of doubt' rather than a 'felt-sense', which is a more contemporary term. Either way, the point is that this perplexity or doubt is experienced as an almost physical sensation. This kind of questioning is not an intellectual exercise but something that seems – as I said yesterday – to penetrate into the marrow of your bones and the pores of your skin.

To give a rather mundane example, it's like losing your car keys. I'm always careful to put my car keys in the same pocket of my jacket. But it has happened that when I go back to my car after having done the shopping, I put my hand into my pocket to get the keys only to find that they're not there. And I think, 'That's odd'. So I put my hand into the other pocket, but they're not there either. And so, presumably with the expectation that two hundred grams of metal will miraculously manifest *ex nihilo*, I put my hand back into the pocket where I've already looked, only to find that they're still not there. After a while, having fruitlessly searched in all sorts of unlikely places on my person, I come to the reluctant conclusion that I don't know where the hell they are.

That sense of utter bafflement has two notable consequences. First, it leaves the mind blank – it comes to a stop, you've exhausted all possibilities. 'Huairang was speechless' as the text says. And second, it provokes a deep visceral questioning: *'Where are they?'* or simply a wordless, open-mouthed perplexity. Such questioning is no detached intellectual enquiry. It stems from your heart and soul, from the very flesh of experience, and leaves you standing bereft and bewildered in a car park with a bag of groceries in your arms. Questioning can engage the whole of us in a palpably physical way.

In meditation we seek to sustain this sensation of questioning in our bodies. This enquiry is an embodied enquiry, and the sitting and walking practices are repeated reminders to come back to the body again and again. Initially, when we ask the question 'What is this?' it might seem to have relatively little purchase on how we feel in our bodies, in fact it might seem that we are just engaging in a curious mental exercise. It may not grab us viscerally at all. But over time, as the meditation brings us into a quieter, calmer, more lucid frame of attention, when we ask 'What is this?' it slowly begins to resonate and reverberate through the whole of us.

Far more important than the words of the question is the psychosomatic resonance that the question evokes, the feeling of questioning that we sense in our guts. Sometimes it is suggested that you ask the question from the *tantien*, a point three finger-widths below your navel, which is described in traditional Chinese anatomy. I don't think we have to get that precise, but the point is that we pose this question with our guts, with our stomach, rather than with our heads.

The sitting, walking and bowing that we will be doing throughout this week all bring our attention slowly further down into the lower regions of our body. I think this takes place in most forms of meditation. If, for example, you practise body-sweeping as taught in the Goenka tradition of Vipassanā, that has a very similar effect.[15] Any prolonged practice of sitting or walking meditation, as well as doing tai chi or yoga: they are all exercises in embodiment, which are completely compatible with what we will be doing here. For some of you those practices might work better at getting you 'into your body', and so I'd encourage you to do them in conjunction with the Sŏn practice if you wish. The main point is to develop a much more grounded awareness and then to infuse that awareness with a deep puzzlement and curiosity. Learn to be surprised that you're embodied, to be astonished that you're an embodied creature in a physical world of sights, sounds, smells, tastes, touches, sensations and so on.

I don't think it's just a western problem that we spend so much time living in our heads. It seems to be a feature of being human. Otherwise, back in seventh century China teachers would not have placed so much emphasis on embodiment. There would have been no need to do this if people didn't feel themselves to be in some way disembodied. So we're not just engaging in a practice that might serve as a valuable corrective to our cerebral modern culture. We're coming to terms with a far broader human tendency to be disembodied, which has probably been the case at all periods in history. Even in fifth century BCE India Gotama says, 'Go to a forest, sit at the root of a tree, pay attention to your breathing'. He presumably gave this instruction because even then people felt cut off from nature, trees, and their breath. Otherwise, why would he have said it?

Now once you begin to sense this questioning or perplexity in a more somatic way, you don't need to keep repeating the words of the question. You simply become more conscious of your perplexed sense of being here at all, in a way that enhances your awareness of being a human creature in this world. It doesn't have to be thought of as anything particularly Sŏn or Buddhist. It's about becoming conscious of another way of being in this world. Some of you might have picked up that I'm using the kind of phenomenological language you find in the work of Martin Heidegger. Heidegger too placed great emphasis on this kind of questioning. For him, such questioning was not just an intellectual activity that went on in the head. At the very end of his essay on technology he says: 'Questioning is the piety of thinking' – *die Frömmigkeit des Denkens*.[16] Yes, piety – there's something almost religious (in the best sense of the word) about this questioning. There's a humility. There's a kind of awe, wonder. A sense of uncanniness. A sort of reverence.

For those of you who have not done this sort of meditation practice before, just a couple of caveats. One: don't just repeat the question as though it were a mantra. It's important to spend as much time as you need to settle into a still, focused attention. And you might do this just by concentrating on the breath or doing some other meditation you may be familiar with that helps you get grounded. Once you feel grounded and still, then gently ask the question 'What is this?'. But pay more attention to the silence that follows the posing of the question. Listen carefully with your inner ear for whatever may arise in response to that question. Yet without any expectation or idea as to what that might be. Be completely without any plan. Be on guard against thinking: 'Oh, I'm practising Sŏn. I'm going to have a satori-like experience any minute now.' Put all of that out of your mind and just try to be as intimate and as present and as deeply serious as you can – without getting tense and agitated – about the question of your own life, the puzzle of your own existence.

Monday evening

TALK

The three symbols of awakening

Martine Batchelor

Tonight I'll discuss what it means when we bow three times towards the statues of either the Buddha or the bodhisattva of compassion at the back of the hall. Stephen presented more of a Tibetan understanding of offering incense, water and a candle. But from a Korean Sŏn point of view, these three offerings that we place on the altar represent awakening. Each of them (incense, water, candle) evokes a different aspect of awakening – of what we're trying to develop as we practise meditation, as we cultivate the path as a whole.

Let's start with incense, which spreads its fragrance while at the same time disappearing, even as it spreads its perfume everywhere. The incense doesn't say, 'Oooh, I don't like that lot over there – I'll just head in the opposite direction'. No, it spreads itself equally. So it represents two aspects of awakening: selflessness – giving something while disappearing; and bestowing equally.

We often talk about not-self, selflessness, emptiness. But what does it mean? When we hear the term 'selflessness' we may gain the impression that it means we need to disappear, that at the end of the retreat there'll just be a puff of smoke on the cushion! Or it might mean that you must not exist! Actually selflessness isn't about that, it's not about disappearing. Selflessness is looking at how much *selfing* I do? How do I self? How self-centred am I? For some strange reason each of us feels like the centre of the universe. Possibly it's more the case that each of us is the centre of her/his own universe, not of the universe as such. Not everything comes back to 'me'.

And that's interesting. Sometimes we say, 'Ah! It's my fault!' But is it really our fault? I mean, did we *actually* make a mistake? At other times we think, 'Oh! It's because of me that this great thing happened!'. Or, 'It's because of me that this bad thing happened!'. Sometimes this is so, but sometimes it isn't true. The idea of 'self-lessness' is inviting us to look first at 'How do we self?'. In the last two days you might have had some experiences of selfing. To an extent selfing arises from thoughts. During the last two days, I presume, you might have been noticing that you've been think-ing. Though possibly not all of you. (Recently I taught on a retreat where I kept talking about thoughts. A retreatant came to me and said, 'You know, when I meditate I don't have any thoughts! Is this a problem?'. I replied, 'No, not at all. This is fine!'. But this isn't what happens to most people on a retreat.)

When we sit in meditation, thoughts are one of the things that will pull us away from the anchor. Thoughts in themselves aren't doing it, but we need to notice what they're about. For me this is fascinating. When I was a nun in Korea and practised asking, 'What is this?', I became aware of my thoughts. This is what I mean by cultivating awareness indirectly. In Korea the teachers generally don't mention mindfulness. Rather, they keep talking about questioning, and the sensation of doubt. That is their *leitmotif*. But as I was asking 'What is this?' I suddenly became aware of my thoughts, and that all my thoughts referred back to *me*! Look at me! I exist! I became acutely aware of my self-interest. It accounted for around 95 per cent of my thoughts, I'd say. This discovery made me realise, 'Oh! That's what meditation is about!'. To me now, that's what selflessness is about. Not about disappearing, but seeing a little of the selfing – the self-centredness – dissolve.

There are two different types of thoughts we can notice in meditation, I feel. The first type revolves around selfing; it's about *me* in many different ways: good me, bad me, look at me. Another kind of thought is creative functioning. When we sit and walk in meditation, we're not trying to *stop* thinking. Instead, we're trying to open up some space within it, so that over time the selfing disappears and we're left with the creative functioning. We exist; we don't have to think about existing. Meditation homes in on experiencing our existing, and on knowing that process as fully as we can. In this way we don't have to spend so much time thinking about existing, or insisting on our existence.

A lot of research on meditation is going on nowadays. Among other aspects it focuses on the resting state of the brain, and shows that the resting state is not especially restful. Recently I participated in one of these research projects, lying in an fMRI scanner with the researcher telling me to just let my mind be, *but don't meditate! Don't think anything specific, just be!* I found it very tough trying to occupy what they call this resting state of the brain without meditating, because this was trying to create something.

The researchers found that people who have meditated for a long time can really enter a resting state of the brain. But then it is very hard for them to enter a non-restful resting state of the brain. There's a little conundrum here!

When we experience selflessness, unnecessary selfing peters out. Of course there needs to be a little bit of selfing: if I don't think about myself who is going to think about me? But how much selfing do we need?

Selflessness is not about disappearing, but functioning in a more creative way. If you have less self-centredness – let's say it comes down to fifty per cent of your thinking – then you have fifty per cent for others. This is an important part of the practice of selflessness. It's not so much about forgetting one's self; rather, it's through reducing our self-centredness that we can live wisely other-centred. In this way we can live for others as much as we live for ourselves. If we're thinking about ourselves less, we'll have more space to encounter the others for themselves, not just in terms of what we might want or hope to get from them. And then we can have an *authentic* encounter, a meeting where something more can happen. The beauty of selflessness is that it helps us to meet our environment, other people and animals, in a much more open and creative way.

Once again: that image of the incense connects us to a crucial aspect of awakening by spreading everywhere to the same degree. Even though we tend to favour people because they like us, or because they're fun, or because we appreciate their qualities, or because they're just easy to get on with.

But what about people who are a little difficult, unpleasant, who might trigger disagreeable feelings in us? They have to live with themselves all the time, but we usually have only to talk to them on the phone or meet them for a few hours. They are suffering, just like we're suffering. Can we open our hearts to them as well?

It's easy to be nice to little bunnies. You've no doubt all seen the rabbits here. I haven't gone out of the house yet, but I will one day, and very likely I'll see the rabbits. They're so cute. But I'm sure if you planted a vegetable garden and they ate all your carrots you might look at the little bunnies in a different way. Or possibly, at the end of the retreat, if you're hungry you might also look at them in a different way, but we won't go there...

Be that as it may, it's through that practice of selflessness that our heart, our love, our compassion can extend our limits in a creative, wise way. And the creative, wise way doesn't imply, 'I must love everybody to the same degree all the time; I must be selfless to the same degree all the time'. Not at all. We must look at the conditions: sometimes I might have to take more care of myself, while at other times I might have to take care more of others. At still other times I can be more even-handed. So within this selflessness there abides wisdom and creativity.

The next symbolic offering is a candle. We light a candle and two things happen. First, similarly to the incense, the candle begins to disappears as it burns; but it takes much more time doing so than the incense. Secondly, until we light it, the candle is opaque. But by contrast, when we do light it, it becomes illuminated and illuminating, and that's integral to our practice. It enables us to illuminate ourselves, and also shines a light for others. That's why the experiential inquiry, the questioning, is so important: it helps us to develop brightness and clarity.

The practice isn't just about being calm; it's also about be-coming lucid, bright, and seeing clearly what's going on. We can see the questioning as a technique – 'I sit here, I walk, I ask "What is this?"'. Or we can see this question as a way of being in the world, a way of questioning in a stable and open manner. This practice will help us to avoid jumping to conclusions, that is, hastily defining, limiting, and fixing our perceptions – habits that once served the evolutionary purpose of survival in a hostile environment. In that survival mode I have to assess very quickly whether these people are dangerous or not, whether this place is safe or not, whether this food is edible or not. Survival mode employs hasty categories: safe versus unsafe place; dangerous versus harmless people; healthy versus contaminated food. We categorise our experience quite automatically in this way. The practice of questioning helps us to balance out these hasty judgements and counteract the tendency to generalise too quickly.

As I said at the beginning: we're living here in silence, there are fifty of us here, and very quickly we categorise people and decide, 'hmmm, good one', 'hmmm, not so sure about that one'. At first, that's what we do. But under the influence of the questioning practice, we start to dissolve those quick perceptions, generalisations and categorisations. Then we can start to ask questions: 'Is this true? Is it always true?'

Another question I've found very useful is, 'How long is this going to last?' This question can arise after a day or two, according to how we feel things are going. This morning I was sitting in meditation and time seemed to go especially slowly. I was sitting there, and I couldn't see the clock, so I thought, 'Hmmm, my body and mind are aching, and the special taste of meditation isn't coming'. So the session seemed to drag out, and I could have jumped to the conclusion that this retreat is going to be a long one. But I didn't think that. Instead I just thought, 'Mmm, that's interesting, that's how it feels'. And then this afternoon, at 2.30, I sat again, and the taste of meditation just arose.

As my teacher said: when meditation is going well you have the impression it's just like pushing a boat over ice. You push a boat on ice and it moves very easily. When it's difficult you get the impression you're trying to drag a cow to drink when she doesn't want to move. This afternoon, my meditation was like pushing that boat over ice, and it glided. I was sitting and it was nice and flowing, and I had the impression that the sit was much shorter, even though it's the same time span! And so this might lead to the opposite impression: 'Oh it's fantastic! This is a great retreat! Every day is going to be like this!'. Or we might be experiencing pain, or we may be bombarded by thoughts, and we might start thinking 'Aïe, aïe, aïe, if I'm going to have this amount of pain every day, it's going to be really tough'. But generally it changes.

When we start to generalise in this way, we amplify our expectations so easily, and the questioning can be useful as a way of counteracting that amplifying effect. We might ask, 'How long is it going to last?' or 'What is going to help change happening?'. Such questions help us to notice how our perceptions change according to the shifting conditions we encounter as the days pass and our energy levels fluctuate.

A basic starting point is that we're not trying to reach a certain state – any particular experience. Especially when we sit in meditation, we have a tendency to wait for something special to happen. It may happen, but not so often. This emphatically doesn't mean you're not practising. You are practising! You are cultivating, but the effect is relatively subtle.

One way to explore the effect of the practice is to check in on how you're feeling at the end of a sitting, or at the end of a walking period. You might feel a little change, a sort of relaxing inwardly. The effect of the walking practice can differ. I love this Sŏn walking at an ordinary pace together inside the hall. I don't know if it works for you in the same way as for me, but at the end of the walking, when I sit I experience a sort of *zinging* effect! Where I feel really bright and alert. So we'll experience slightly different effects from the sitting, from the walking, from the walking outside, from the questioning, as we practise.

Importantly, when we're asking the question we're trying

to anchor, as well as cultivate a sensation of questioning. Through that process we start to see things more clearly. It's not as if mega insights occur, but we're seeing more clearly when we inquire into our experience: 'How is my body?' 'How is my heart?' 'What is going on in my mind?' 'How is it to just sit here?' We're getting closer to what we're actually experiencing instead of losing touch with it by commenting on it and trying to explain it. We're trying to stay just with the experience as it arises. Within the framework of just sitting there, and through asking the question or coming back to the breath, or whatever it is we're using as an anchor, we have all these opportunities to come back to this whole moment and to experience ourselves as multi-perspectival.

Often we may feel we're becoming a thought, a feeling, a sensation, a sound, or whatever it might be. These different things exist, but we can't reduce ourselves to any one of them. For me, this realisation is about becoming much clearer, seeing more from that multifaceted perspective – experiencing that we're a *flow* of inner conditions meeting outer conditions, and realising this again and again.

Then there's the important illuminating aspect. It helps us to become not only more stable, open, quiet and clear, but also more compassionate. Because it removes and dissolves certain obstacles to encountering the other, encountering the environment. If we're clearer, and if we're less self-centred, we can meet the other in a much more creative way, so that we can mutually benefit each other. I know you are in silence here, so you won't have that opportunity right now. But at the end of the retreat on Saturday morning the silence will be broken, and then you can try it out.

When we have a conversation with somebody, we might start with a little discussion. Does it become an argument, or does it become a dialogue? It becomes an argument when we cling to our idea; if the other person questions our idea we then feel they're questioning us. And if we feel that, then their questioning is very painful – when actually they're just questioning our idea, not our identity.

What happens if the discussion becomes a dialogue? The two individuals – and this is the beauty of encountering another – have different perceptions, different perspectives, different ideas. If we meet in an open manner, in an illuminated/illuminating manner, we can benefit from each other. When melding and exploring these two perceptions we can often generate a higher understanding, because each of us can bring something to the occasion.

When we have a discussion, what is it about? It might be: 'I'm going to tell it like it is! I must convince this person!'. The first time we tell them, they don't get it. So the second time we say it louder, but I'm not sure it will have a greater effect. On the other hand, if we really share, if we really come together, then it can be illuminating for both. Each bringing something which can become something bigger. I find it wonderful when I have a discussion like that. It feels so enlivening, so illuminating both for myself and for the other person. And we can surprise ourselves, 'Oh! I never thought of it that way!'.

The last symbolic offering is water, which has two aspects. One is that it flows. In the Zen tradition they say, 'It flows, but it doesn't flow up… generally it flows down.' Often when we think about awakening, we think we're going to climb to the top of the mountain. And then I'll be on top of the mountain, and I'll say 'Hey! Look at me! I'm awakened! Become my disciple!'.

I don't live in Totnes any more, but it used to be fun when I did. Every few years, a new guru appeared on the high street, and suddenly everyone you knew would be following him and using the same expressions! As against that, I like the idea that water flows down, moving ever deeper. Often people think of awakening, as becoming like a Christmas tree, as if we sit here all lit up like a Christmas tree, hovering above the cushion. However, a more helpful understanding might be that the practice helps us to become ordinary – as in becoming fully human. We discover our good qualities, as well as our difficult qualities, and creatively engage with them. Without needing to be special.

When I was young, I always wanted to be special. When I became a nun in Korea I reached the summit of being special: *top du top* as we say in French. I was *unique* among 120 million people – that's really special – because there were 60 million Koreans and 60 million French people, and I was the only Korean Buddhist French nun. But then I stopped being a nun and I stopped living in Korea, so I became un-special. At the beginning I would go for a walk in the village and I would feel weird. I thought, 'Why am I feeling weird?' and then I realised because no one looked at me especially because I don't look foreign, and I don't wear funny clothes, and I just look like everybody else. Then I started to enjoy not being special, and really enjoying being ordinary.

That's where this practice takes us – really appreciating and creatively engaging with this flow of conditions. Right here, right now, meeting this environment. And that's what the water flowing down is about.

The second aspect of water is that it's adaptable, flexible. Whatever receptacle you put it in, it will adopt that shape: round, square, rectangular, flat. This is the beauty of the practice, that it helps us to become more flexible, especially this type of meditation with questioning.

Different methods can have different effects. Take the example of focusing on the breath: as long as you're not asthmatic, it can be very useful for calming the body. Being aware of the body can be very grounding. Listening to sound can be opening. Cultivating lovingkindness can orient us towards love, kindliness. And questioning is a great method for cultivating flexibility.

I'm not saying it's the best method; it's only one method among others. But it's a really good method in terms of flexibility, because we have this tendency to define, to fix: 'This is it. This is like that. It's like this.' We have a tendency to be very definite, and we want other people to be definite. Questioning helps us to be more flexible, to counteract rigidity, to bring that defining impulse back to its creative function rather than leave it in its hasty, reactive mode. Questioning can make us more creative so that we give ourselves more choices. Thus we can see that part of the practice is about 'making a creative choice'. Without that possibility we can make bad choices: 'I hate you, I'll choose this!' or 'I hate that, I'll choose this!'.

I'm talking about creative, illuminated or illuminating choice – what we can reach for when we come back to the anchor, to sitting here, to the walking, to eating, to the task at hand. At that point we come back to this multiplicity, this multi-faceted perspective. The practice asks us to be flexible: flexible for ourselves, flexible for others. As we sit in meditation and we come back to the anchor again and again, sometimes this perspective arises by itself, sometimes we remind ourselves, sometimes we come back to ourselves,

There are many different ways to make that choice to come back to the anchor, and every time we do so (especially with questioning) we're cultivating this flexibility, this adaptability. It will then help us to be more creative, instead of thinking there is just this or just that. We start to realise, 'Oh yes, I could do it this way, or possibly I could do it that way, or possibly I'll wait and see!' One of the mantras I find useful in daily life is, 'Let's see what happens'. Often we've barely started something, yet we've already decided 'It must be like this! It has to be like that, or else!'. Instead, I like to think, 'Oh, let's try it. Let's see what happens.' Of course I want to take matters in a certain direction, but I'm not defining the outcome already, as in 'It's going to be good, it's going to be bad, it's going to be like this, it's going to be like that.' Rather, I just say to myself, 'Let's see what happens'.

Recently I was travelling to Mexico, Los Angeles and North Carolina. Before reaching each of these places I was thinking, 'Let's see what happens'. Approaching Mexico, an official announcement says, 'Be careful, you might get zika, dengue fever,' and I don't know what else. But I thought to myself, after hearing this announcement: 'Let's see what happens'. It turned out to be so cold there were no mosquitoes.

Then I travel to North Carolina, and the retreat centre I'm heading for is barely finished. At the end of the retreat I say, 'But at least the meditation room was really nice'. And my hosts answer, 'You should have seen it the day before you arrived!'. Apparently a week earlier one wall didn't exist and the roof had caved in, but in that week they'd transformed it. These people inspired me, really going for it so we could all do this retreat.

So the offering of water symbolises this flexibility. The creative choices we can make when we encounter life afresh, which often surprises us.

Tuesday morning

Effortless effort

Martine Batchelor

This morning I'd like to explore various aspects of our practice. First, I want to go further into the idea of *anchoring and questioning*: how we're trying to cultivate the two of them together in our practice, as well as establishing a balance between the two. We can try to do so with the questioning in the first instance. But our approach can also apply to other meditative focuses, for instance breath awareness. We can approach them as well in terms of anchoring and questioning.

I want to read two quotes which to me evoke these two basic themes of the Korean Sŏn tradition. The first quote starts like this:

> *If one remains in deep calm without being aware it means sinking into dullness...*

Here we find two elements: *anchoring/questioning*, and *calm/ brightness*. Sometimes we associate meditation with being calm, and we follow the conventional axiom that the aim of the meditation is to become and stay calm. But here's our quote telling us that if we remain in deep calm without being aware, we're sinking into dullness. We have to stay aware that we need to balance these two elements of calmness/energy and stillness/brightness. Of course we want to be calm, and stability is really helpful, but by itself it's not enough. If we're simply calm but low in energy, we can slip into dullness.

If for example you use the breath as a way to calm yourself, and you're tired at the same time – oops, you might find yourself becoming sluggish. At that point you can brighten yourself up by bringing in questioning. In this way, the energy can return to your sit without disturbing the calm that you've cultivated.

And that is why the second part of the first quote from the Sŏn tradition goes on:

> *...and if one remains aware without being calm it means becoming entangled in one's thoughts.*

So we also need to balance awareness or brightness with calmness, as too much awareness or brightness can lead to mental agitation. Once when I was in Korea I did a three-month retreat with nuns. They couldn't believe the fact that I never slept on the cushion. They themselves would sit and very quickly fall fast asleep, while I'd stay awake the whole time. So they finally came to me and wanted to know my secret: what was I doing not to fall asleep on the cushion? 'I can't fall asleep because I have too many thoughts', I replied. Many of us follow this pattern – if we don't have enough calmness then we're apt to be taken over by habitual thoughts. So if there is just brightness without calmness, it could divert too much energy towards the thinking process. Then comes the last part of this particular quote:

> *If one is in a state of being neither aware nor calm then one is not only entangled in thoughts but also submerged in dullness.*

You might experience this state of mind from time to time, more likely after lunch. Hence it's vital to strike a balance between calmness and brightness. Undoubtedly it's more agreeable to have less thoughts and more calm, but we also need to acknowledge that at times we're not getting the balance right. We might find ourselves distracted for whatever reason, or we might be a little sleepy, and we cannot help ourselves. At the same time we could bring attention to that: 'Oh, right now I'm distracted!', but in the midst of the distracting thoughts we could just sit there with this particular thought too, and like everything else it will pass at some point. Or you might start feeling bright and then – ooh! – you feel sleepy, then you also accept that state, and finally at some point that too will pass.

There are two aspects to creative awareness. One is acceptance – let's see how long this lasts; and the other is transformation – at what point do I need to do something about this? With distraction we could come back to the anchoring. If we really feel sleepy we might want to straighten the back, open the eyes wide, look up towards the ceiling and ask a few times, 'Who is sitting here? Who is asking the question? Who is breathing?' and that might be enough to wake us up, so we can come back to a suitable anchor.

Whenever we practise meditation we have these two choices. First, what is it I accept, and wait for it to pass (because it must pass at some point)? Second, at what point do I do something which might help to change it?

Here comes the second quote from the Sŏn tradition:

Clear awareness and deep calm are beneficial. But clear awareness with delusion will not work.

Once again we're reminded that it's not just a question of being aware. We're not just trying to stare at reality, we're not trying to become radar monitors. Rather, we're developing a certain quality of awareness which (as I said yesterday) is illuminated or illuminating, so the awareness possesses clarity and brightness. We're aiming for a certain quality of consciousness, of attention, of awareness.

Deep calm and clear awareness are appropriate. But deep calm with absent-mindedness is not appropriate.

You might find yourself calm, but in that calmness do you have some brightness, do you have some clarity? Or is the calm leading to vagueness, or sometimes we could even say dissociation? We could be calm, but if this were a calmness detached from reality, then one would not be experiencing a multi-faceted perspective. Certain practices in various religions help you to have this dissociative calmness, even in the Buddhist tradition, and it could be beneficial in some ways. But if we want to bring our meditation practice into daily life, the calm we want to develop has to embrace being here in a very clear way. That way we're saying yes to calmness, but brightness must infuse the calmness. We must not retreat into vagueness, unclarity and dissociation. The quote in question finishes with:

How can any delusion arise if calm doesn't let in any distraction, and awareness doesn't leave any room for unskilful thinking?

We can't follow this advice all the time. It's not a recipe. If we use all the ingredients one hundred percent of the time, then our meditation soufflé will be perfect! But we know from our experience of soufflé that the outcome depends on conditions, and it's the same with meditation.

How can any delusion arise if calm doesn't let in any distraction?

What is being pointed out here is that the function of anchoring is to bring us back to creative functioning.

We're not trying to stop thought itself, nor the thinking process. Rather, we're working with the quality of the thought. What is it we're being distracted by? Let's take an example: sometimes one of the things people do in meditation is what I call 'rumination'. So we start a sit, we're here, totally fine. And then suddenly we remember something bad somebody did to us: they said this, they did this – how terrible! In this way we bring the pain of the past into the present, and then we often jump into the future and plot revenge. 'I'll meet them and I'll get them!'. Such a compassionate activity in meditation!

Yet we can question the whole process. 'Do I need to do this? Can I leave the past where it is? Can I learn from it, but can I leave it there?'. In that imagined future encounter the other person isn't going to follow my script, so it's not going to work. Not only that, my script is also vengeful, which isn't compassionate. If we think vengeful thoughts, the Buddha pointed out, we're likely to act on them. But if we can bring ourselves back to the only thing we can do, which is to practise now, then we'll be able to meet the other person with more calmness later on. Thus we're cultivating calmness not just for its own sake, but to help us make skilful choices in everyday life.

I don't know if you've had this experience, but let's say we have to write an email in which you have to take up a difficult subject with someone. I don't have to do this often, but when I do the process unfolds like this: first I think about the contents of the email, and it may sound a little nasty. So I reflect on the wording of the email a second time, and its gets a little softer. And usually by the fourth revisit I think, 'Yes, that's the right way to say it!' By anchoring, by coming back, we can achieve this wise creative functioning, instead of feeding what is going to be harmful, what is going to be confusing. The quote also says:

Awareness doesn't leave any room for unskilful thinking.

So the two aspects go together: the calmness will dissolve the power of the habitual thoughts; and the clarity – the awareness – is going to identify the type of thought in question. Sometimes we have a creative thought while sitting in meditation, which is totally fine, and we can then continue to develop our understanding as we go on thinking creatively.

When I was sitting in Korea for ten hours a day, by the end of the day I'd often feel a lot of pain. Sometimes I'd just sit with the pain, which was difficult. But sometimes I could go inside the pain and experience its emptiness. At such times I had clear awareness. This is what I call *meditative creative thinking*. We see something very clearly, something we've never seen in this way before – never thought about in this way before.

We think about it a little, and then at some point the creativity fades and we reflect, 'I must remember this, tell all my friends about it. I'm going to write a book about it,' or whatever, but we usually let it be. And so it is with awareness. 'Oh yeah! This is a creative thought,' we note. The same awareness empowers us to reflect, 'Ooh, this is a vengeful thought! Is this where I want to go?'.

Another habitual routine we can get caught up in goes like this: we experience an unpleasant thought which leads us into self-pity: 'Poor me, poor me!'. We have that initial unpleasant thought, and within five minutes we're in a deeply unpleasant place. It's similar to waiting for somebody who's late. It's nine o'clock and, they're not here. Then it's ten past nine. 'S/he doesn't love me.' By twenty past nine it's, 'Nobody loves me!' and by nine thirty it's 'I hate the world!'. In this way we can see how a thought can lead us to a dark place. Do we really want to go there? Being able to say no and let go is what the awareness is for.

When we practise, we're cultivating anchoring and brightness together. We can do this with questioning of course, and we can also help ourselves with the breath. Another method mentioned in Korean Sŏn texts, one associated with the bodhisattva of compassion, is *listening*. We can bring some listening meditation into our practice, including for its own sake. By this I mean that we can place sound in the foreground and everything else in the background; or we could even choose what I call 'stacking up'. For example we can place the question in the foreground, a bit of listening just behind it, and then the rest of experience in the background. Personally I've found that if I ask the question together with a little listening, I gain the impression that my questioning of the experience of the moment goes deeper.

Listening meditation is not a scientific analysis. We're not making a list, not sitting there thinking, 'Okay, I heard a bird, now I hear this, now I hear that!'. Instead, we're just using listening to sounds as an anchor. And we can use it in two ways. We can sit with open awareness – we're just aware of the space in which the sound occurs. Or we can become aware of the most prominent sound. Of course, we're not sitting there asking, 'What is the most prominent sound? That's the one I'm going to!'. By then it's gone! It's more a question of which sounds attracts your attention.

We sit in meditation and we might hear a bird. Next we might hear a cough. Next we might hear an unidentifiable sound

– that's an interesting one! When we practise listening meditation, we're listening to the sound for itself, and as far as possible we avoid commenting on the sound. Of course as soon as we hear a sound, we might know what it is. 'I know it's a bird!' But we're not trying to name birds, we're trying to be with the sound itself. And that's why, when there's a sound that we don't know, we see how much we want to know. We're meaning-making animals – we want to know what it is! We're thinking: 'Is it inside? Is it outside? What's going on?'. But can we stay there, just listening to the sound?

As we listen to sounds, we can observe how they arise and pass away. We can also note, if a sound continues, how it changes within itself. In this way we can practise listening meditation, as if we're listening to the music of life.

There's another way in which we can use different anchors in a complementary way. In the foreground we continue with questioning, very much within the body, trying to keep the question embedded rather than floating, so the whole body and mind are asking the question, but without tension. At the same time, there can be some listening so we feel more embedded in the experience, and then all other aspects of experience fill in the background. It's up to each of us to see which approach will suit us best.

If you're more used to following the breath, you could stay with the breath, then open to sound, then return to the breath. Again, these practices complement each other. Or you can stay with the breath, and then from time to time drop the question into the mind. Or you can stay with sound, just listening, and then from time to time drop in the question. On a retreat we're exploring. We can explore the posture, or the method, to see what works – and what doesn't work.

When we practise walking meditation, we can continue to repeat the question, 'What is this?' silently, inwardly. Or we can match the question with the rhythm of our steps with a little bit of the sound stacked up behind it. What can be fun (unless we get obsessed with it) is hearing and focusing in on the sounds of our shuffling on the carpet. It makes for a wonderful piece of music. But of course there are also the sounds coming from outside.

Now let me turn to something very important in the Korean Sŏn tradition – the notion of *effortless effort*. There's a big difference between the effort we bring to sitting every day for ten, twenty, thirty minutes or more on the one hand, and on the other hand the effort we have to put in on a retreat when we're sitting throughout the day for days on end.

We have a strange relationship with effort. Often we think we've really put in effort if we get an effect. So we mix up effort and effect, and we have to be careful about that. When we try to do something, even if we don't seem to get the effect we're expecting, it doesn't mean we're not trying.

Also, when we put in effort we become tense. This is because we tend to think of efforting as tensing up the whole body and mind if we're to achieve anything. We have to watch out for that assumption, while acknowledging that we need to put out enough effort if our energy and practice are not to slump. It's a bit like our way of watching television. In meditation, we're watching the inner TV, one might say. We tend not to sit upright in a good posture in front of the TV, preferring to slump on a sofa this way or that, trying to find a more comfortable position, until often we end up lying supine in a bundle.

Sitting in meditation here, we need to put in a certain effort just to sit still. If we don't put out enough effort we slouch, which isn't good; but if we have too much effort then we're too upright. We need to find a comfortable posture for the body, but also for the mind. Sometimes I find that I'm sitting, clenching my jaw to question more intently. So I often check for that tendency, relax the jaw, and go back to effortless effort.

We can't have the same effortless effort all the time, because sometimes we have more energy, while at other times we have less. So sometimes we need to summon up a little more energy to generate more brightness, while at other times we need a little more relaxation. This goes for both the body and the mind. From time to time it's helpful to ask, 'How am I efforting?'. Sometimes it feels as if the meditation is unfolding by itself, and that really feels like 'effortless effort'.

So pay attention to your changing energy and effort levels. It's like walking along an undulating path – the effort isn't the same going up as it is going down. There's a cycling path along an old railway line near our house: it's fairly flat, but not always so. At times when cycling along it one does have to pedal strongly, even though the track looks flat. It's a little like that with meditation. Sometimes we just let it happen, and sometimes we have to bring up more energy. But within that, we can also achieve effortless effort.

Tuesday evening

Good snowflakes: they don't fall anywhere else

Stephen Batchelor

This talk is called 'Good snowflakes: they don't fall anywhere else.' It refers to a kongan – case no. 42 in the collection called the *Blue cliff record*, attributed to a Tang dynasty Sŏn teacher who's known as Layman Pang. He's one of the very few lay people considered to be a Sŏn master of that period. We know hardly anything about him; he had a wife and daughter, both of whom were also considered to be accomplished practitioners. This kongan is presented with hardly any context. The text reads:

> *When Layman Pang left Yaoshan, the monastery had ten Sŏn practitioners accompany him to the gate. The layman pointed to the falling snow and said:*

'Good snowflakes – they don't fall anywhere else'.[17]

That's it: 'Good snowflakes: they don't fall anywhere else'. I've always been struck by this remark, and pondered and meditated on it for many years. As with all kongans, were I now to offer you some explanation of what it means this would miss the point. Kongans are good examples of the distinction between showing and telling. This is one of the mantras of the creative writing world, which you may have come across if you have ever been on workshops or read books in this field. A key injunction to follow when writing is this: 'show, don't tell'. In other words, reveal your story, your characters, your world, don't stand back and explain to the reader what is going on and who the people are. This might sound somewhat obvious, but in practice it is not easy to do.

So when Pang says, 'Good snowflakes: they don't fall anywhere else', he's showing us something. It doesn't require an explanation. To explain it would be to tell what it means, rather than to allow the image to speak for itself. 'What is this thing and how did it get here?' 'The cypress tree in the courtyard.' 'Three pounds of flax.' These are all ways of *showing* you something. And that showing can have the effect of bringing the mind to a stop. That is where the power of these teachings and stories resides. They bring the calculating mind to a halt. You are left just with an image. And that image is something you can then attend to and ponder, allowing it to come alive in a way that may be surprising and revealing.

This approach, I feel, is very much at the heart of Sŏn practice. Let me offer some images drawn from our own culture that might help these 'good snowflakes' speak to us in the language of our time – and even provoke in us a similar effect as it did on monks in Tang China. For me, this kongan evokes a very fundamental sense of this world in which we find ourselves. This world into which we were thrown at birth, of which we gradually grew aware as our consciousness and language became more refined, as we began to emerge as a distinct person with a coherent history, the sense of a future, and a foreboding about our own death.

To do this, I will take some images of the world as it is presented to us through the natural sciences. I'm not a scientist and have not been trained in the sciences. In fact, I find a great deal of biology, physics and chemistry very hard to understand. I'm not 'wired' to think in that way. At school I always opted for the arts rather than the sciences. I found what we were taught in science classes dull, unengaging. Added to which, I could never get my head around the mathematics. Yet today when I read popular books, listen to a radio programme or watch documentaries about the discoveries of the natural sciences, it often evokes in me feelings that might best be described as religious. I find the sheer scale and vastness of space and time overwhelming. And I become acutely aware of the poignancy, the utter contingency of existence. Contingency means that, on the one hand, something arises contingent on other conditions, which, in turn, are contingent on yet other conditions, ad infinitum. And, on the other hand, we make 'contingency plans' because we realise that what we prepare ourselves for might suddenly get thrown off course by circumstances we hadn't foreseen coming into play.

Such notions of contingency are very close, I feel, to what the Buddha meant by *paṭiccasamuppāda*, usually translated as 'dependent origination' or 'conditioned arising'. Remember, in the early suttas the Buddha says that the person who sees such conditioned arising sees the dharma, and the person who sees the dharma sees conditioned arising. So there's something very much at the core of the Buddha's teaching which has to do with waking up to what I would call the utterly contingent nature of experience.

'Good snowflakes – they don't fall anywhere else' is, perhaps, how the Chinese imagination understands this teaching.

This very concrete, vivid image from the natural world, taking place at a specific moment in time, shows us contingency – far more potently than the rather abstract descriptions that we find in the *Abhidharma* and other traditional Buddhist commentaries. However useful such teachings might be, they operate at a level of abstraction that takes us away from the immediacy of what's happening in a given moment and attempt, instead, to tell us what *paṭiccasamuppāda* means. This conceptual understanding always remains, I feel, two or three steps removed from the actuality of any given moment of life itself.

I suspect when I said: 'Good snowflakes: they don't fall anywhere else', you might have found yourself recalling an experience of standing in a white, wintry landscape with snowflakes floating down, in that curious way they have of lazily drifting before eventually coming to settle somewhere. And something that Layman Pang would not have known, but we do know, is that no two snowflakes are ever the same. There's something unique and utterly specific in each of these ephemeral crystallisations of water, contingent on certain temperatures and weather conditions, that fall from the sky, come to rest, and finally dissolve back into water and disappear.

All this occurs in a world that is shot through with such contingency, flux and poignancy. It all 'started' with the so-called Big Bang or, more correctly, a 'singularity,' that is impossible to imagine. For this is something that did not occur anywhere at any time. Thus the commonsensical questions, 'what was there before the Big Bang?' or 'what gave rise to the Big Bang' are meaningless. Because before the Big Bang there was no 'before'. Since both time and space emerged from the Big Bang, it is unintelligible to say that anything occurred before it. Nor did it occur at any place, because not only was there no 'then' 'then', there was also no 'there' 'then'.

In a way that is beyond anything I can conceptually grasp, everything that we experience now, every little atom, every blade of grass, every breath we take, would not have occurred – would not be occurring – had this singularity not erupted and generated this universe. And when we think of the billions of galaxies that make up the universe, we find that we live in one tiny little solar system within one galaxy, the Milky Way, which is likewise made up of billions of other solar systems. When I try to get my mind around the numbers and distances involved, it is simply too much – you just can't do it. It brings the mind to a stop.

The same thing happens when we turn our attention inwards to the neurological structure of the brain. It likewise seems to go on infinitely, except now on a microscopic rather than a macroscopic scale. A few years ago I participated in a conference on Buddhism and consciousness at the Upaya Zen Center in Santa Fe, New Mexico. One of the presenters was the neuroscientist Dr. Richard Davidson, a researcher who has done a great deal of work on investigating the effects of meditation on the brain.[18] As part of his presentation he showed a five-minute video clip, which took us on a slow-moving tour through one square millimetre of a rat's brain. The journey through this 'universe' of neurons, axons, dendrites and so on, was not only beautiful (despite the rather cheesy music that accompanied it) but made you realise that whether you look out into the distant stars or whether you look in to the neurological structure of the brain, you encounter something very similar. In both cases, what you find seems almost endlessly complex and utterly unfathomable, quite incapable of being captured conceptually – at least by my mind.

These vistas evoke, for me, much the same sense of awe and puzzlement as does a kongan. I feel that what the sciences show us is a glimpse into this extraordinary universe, of which we are just tumbling little snowflakes existing for a flash of time: fifty, sixty, seventy years, which in the grand scheme of things is really nothing. And yet here we are.

'What is this and how did it get here?' Asked in the contemplative context of a Sŏn retreat, this question too can awaken a similar quality of perplexity. And to that extent, it reveals the sublimity of ordinary experience: that is, no matter how mundane something might seem, from another perspective it is impossible to pin it down, define it, say what it 'really' is.

This planet was dominated for millions of years by dinosaurs. Then suddenly around 65 million years ago there was a massive meteor impact just off the Yucatán Peninsula in the Gulf of Mexico, which effectively obliterated the dinosaurs, and many other forms of life as well, but at the same time allowed the opportunity for certain little mammals, probably a bit like rats or mice, to have the opportunity to occupy the vacant ecological niches that previously were the domain of the dinosaurs. And it's from these rodent-like creatures that other mammalian life evolved that eventually led to you and me sitting here in Gaia House asking 'What is this?'.

Again, there's something profoundly contingent about all this. If that asteroid had not crashed into the planet, there's no reason (as far as I can tell) that the dinosaurs would not still be roaming around, doing what dinosaurs do, and those little mammals would be doing their best to survive in the cracks and the crevices of the dinosaur world without ending up as mid-morning snack for one of them. But we would not be here. We would simply not have happened. In other words, the fact that human life evolved at all is dependent upon rocks in space circling the sun, which very occasionally crash into other rocks, which wipe out certain life forms that have evolved on those other rocks, thereby bringing a certain line of evolution to an abrupt halt, and thereby creating the conditions for other forms of life to flourish.

In terms of the cosmic timeframe, we are latecomers on the scene. The first human beings anatomically identical to us – who, when naked, would have been indistinguishable from us – first appeared somewhere between a hundred and fifty and two hundred thousand years ago. Which is really just the blink of an eye. And how long we will manage to remain here is anyone's guess.

The fact that all of this has happened seems entirely accidental and arbitrary. This is difficult for human beings to accept. We like to tell ourselves stories that explain how special we are. We invent concepts like 'God' to show how the story of life on earth was designed in such a way that would culminate in humankind, made 'in the image' of God. The idea that humans could actually be a purely contingent and haphazard event we find deeply uncomfortable. We have an instinctive sense that we're so much more than just a pure accident, that there must be some reason for our being here.

Buddhists may not speak of God, but they nonetheless have developed theories of karma, which attempts to explain how over countless lifetimes we have been reaping the results of our previous actions that lead us to getting born in one place rather than another, and as one kind of creature rather than another. This too explains why we exist; it provides reasons that we can get our heads around. It makes us feel that we are meant to be here. According to classical Buddhist theory, this has been going on forever – since 'beginningless time'. But the natural sciences simply don't back that up. We have emerged, it appears, out of purely physical conditions by random mutations and chance.

In principle, I see no reason why Buddhists should have an issue with this explanation of how life evolved; it accords well with the principle of conditioned arising. But I suspect many of them, like their theistic brothers and sisters, find this account rather chilling. It makes them uncomfortable. If everything is the product of chance, rather than the moral consequences of our karma, it cannot account for the dignity and special opportunities of being human. But given what we now know from evolutionary biology, we have little choice, I feel, but to swallow the fact that these pre-modern explanations might simply be wrong. The fact is that we're here and, as far as we know, these material conditions alone are what gave rise to us being here.

Let's bring this even closer to home, and reflect on the contingency of our own specific existence. The contingency of Stephen here, Kate over there, and Jonathan at the rear of the hall. Then imagine going back to the moment at which you were conceived. Your parents were having sex, and your father ejaculated. Then one of his spermatozoa managed to fertilise your mother's ovum, which managed to secure itself to her uterus wall, and grew into a viable embryo that was born nine months later, and – bingo! – there you were.

But just imagine if it had been another of the millions of your dad's spermatozoa that had fertilised the ovum. Would the resultant person still have been Stephen, or Kate, or Jonathan? Would it not have been the equivalent of their twin? It would be someone else, right? Or imagine that you were conceived in your mother's next ovarian cycle. Would that person have been you? No, it would have been someone else.

Or imagine that in the midst of your parents' passionate lovemaking the phone rang. Now that might have been a minor inconvenience for your mum and dad, which got them out of the mood, but the result would be that you didn't get to exist. Maybe it was just a drunk who dialled a wrong number. But their *coitus interruptus* means that you don't happen ... ever. I'm making a bit of a joke of this, but it illuminates well the blunt fact that your own existence is highly haphazard, that it's far more likely that you or I would not have existed at all. We've come into being entirely dependent upon the distant causes of evolution and the more proximate causes of our respective parents' reproductive cells.

And here we are; something profoundly contingent.

Layman Pang said: 'Good snowflake: they don't fall anywhere else'. Instead of snowflakes, we could just as well talk of my father's spermatozoa, my mother's ova, the asteroid smashing into the Yucatán Peninsula, and whatever other contingencies and accidents and chance events might have come along and just nudged the process a few degrees in a different direction. It's highly improbable that human beings exist at all, and yet the curious thing is we take this so totally for granted. We regard our own existence as just an unavoidable given, something that we often feel disinterested in or bored about. We wake up in the morning without giving a moment's thought to all these billions of years of evolution and the extraordinary combination of events that have produced us, and say to ourselves: 'Oh shit. Me again. Another day in Newton Abbot. What's on Netflix tonight?'

Now this is a very odd way to attend to something that is so mind-bogglingly weird. I feel that what the dharma is trying to point to is, as the Buddha put it, 'clearly visible' (*sandiṭṭhiko*). And since he says that the dharma he discovered was conditionality, then this implies that conditionality is clearly visible. Not as an abstract principle only accessible to reason, but in the mundane workings of ordinary life – like the falling of snowflakes. But the Buddha goes on to say that what is clearly visible is also 'hard to see' (*dudaso*). In other words, contingency might be playing itself out right before our eyes, but because we are so preoccupied with being permanent, secure and self-sufficient, we don't see it. Another Sŏn metaphor expresses this paradox well:

We spend our lives like a fish swimming through the oceans in search of water.

The natural sciences render conditionality 'clearly visible' in the most beautiful and vivid way that I can imagine. Frankly, in reading a book on evolutionary biology I get a far more powerful sense of conditioned arising than by poring over a dry Buddhist philosophical treatise on the topic. It doesn't have the same impact at all. Likewise, what draws me to Sŏn is that it prefers concrete images to ideas and concepts. Sŏn teachers urge us to put aside theoretical speculation and ponder instead an image: snowflakes, the cypress tree in the courtyard, three pounds of flax.

Of course, in Tang dynasty China people had no knowledge of evolutionary theory or astrophysics. But I find that our current worldview serves to contextualise the cypress tree in the courtyard in a way that illuminates the traditional Buddhist idea of conditionality by locating it within the interstellar expanses of this universe and our incredibly complex brains. So to ask ourselves 'What is this?' today will inevitably have associations and resonances for us that it could not ever have had for Huineng and Huairang in Tang China.

'What is this thing, and how did it get here?' At one level we can answer this by picturing the Big Bang that leads eventually to Huairang's parents having sex, Huairang getting born, and Huairang saying, 'I think I'll go down to south China to check out that meditation teacher everyone's talking about'. The story points to the same extraordinary reality: this highly contingent, highly fluid, highly temporary, highly interconnected life of which we are just one tiny little pulsing bit. So when I ask myself 'What is this?' in the back of my mind I cannot help but have a sense of the contingency that is revealed through our understanding of the natural world.

This practice also has for me a profoundly aesthetic quality. And here we can learn a great deal from the notion of the sublime that was developed by people like Edmund Burke, Samuel Taylor Coleridge, William Wordsworth and John Keats in the late eighteenth and early nineteenth centuries. For these philosophers and poets too found themselves astonished and overwhelmed by the wonders that were being revealed through the natural sciences.

There's a popular idea still current that the Romantics reacted against the sciences, rejecting its cold, heartless account of the world in favour of a return to immediate feeling and sensory experience. But this view is comprehensively debunked in a very good book by Richard Holmes (the biographer of both Shelley and Coleridge) called *The age of wonder: how the Romantic generation discovered the beauty and terror of science*, which shows how Romanticism was very much an aesthetic, imaginative response to the scientific discoveries that emerged in the wake of the European enlightenment. The Romantics were not opposed to these findings; they were often inspired by them. But as philosophers and poets, rather than physicists, chemists or mathematicians, the language they used was that of the imagination.

Their concept of the sublime, I feel, can likewise help illuminate the kinds of practices we do in meditation, be it mindfulness, Vipassanā or Sŏn. The Romantics famously sought out experiences of the sublime. Coleridge, for example, would go hiking in the Lake District during a violent storm with a bottle of brandy in one pocket and a bottle of laudanum in the other in order to experience the 'suspension of the powers of comparison',[19] which is how he defined the experience of the sublime. The sublime, a term whose use has been debased and trivialised in our time, originally referred to those experiences that *exceeded the capacity for representation*. In other words, there's something about tramping through the countryside in a powerful storm at night – particularly when you're out of your head on opium and brandy – that brings the mind to a stop.

Other examples would be when we're adrift in a little boat on a rough sea or, like Lucretius, lying in a field at night contemplating the vast boundlessness of the sky. There's something about these experiences that can be overwhelming, awe inspiring, and even frightening. No words or ideas can adequately express them. What's going on is simply too much for the everyday mind to grasp, any more than it can grasp what goes on in a square millimetre of a rat's brain, or the Big Bang. The Romantic poets valued such experiences because at such moments they felt most fully alive.

Another characteristic of the sublime, which is discussed in Edmund Burke's *A philosophical inquiry into the origin of our ideas of the sublime and beautiful*, is that these experiences are simultaneously fascinating and terrifying. We find ourselves drawn to the swell of the sea at night in a little boat, to the starry heavens, to the power of a great storm, and yet at the same time that attraction is often qualified by a visceral sense of fear. Paradoxically, the fear and the attraction go hand in hand. This reminds one of Søren Kierkegaard's definition of anxiety, which he understands as a state of attraction and aversion in equal measure. We find the sublime profoundly uncanny and disquieting but at the same time irresistibly attractive.

Now all of this, I think, has many resonances with Buddhist thought. The idea of being stuck in one's ego and its machinations implies that we remain trapped in a very limited outlook on life. It might give us a feeling of security, of being someone important, a sense of having a coherent story in our minds that gives us a handle on what's going on around us. But being caught in such concepts and storylines is exactly what Sŏn practice seeks to dispel. Drop all your Buddhist theories, say the Sŏn masters, and come back to just sitting on the ground experiencing your breath, experiencing your body. Return to the immediacy of life itself.

For me, the practice of meditation is about allowing ourselves to let go of those hesitations, fears and concerns that prevent us from opening ourselves, our hearts and minds, to what we might call the 'everyday sublime'.[20] Because it's not just starry heavens and violent storms that are sublime. When your mind becomes more still, when you become more present, when the habits of your neurotic thinking die down – as they might during a retreat such as this – all this will allow you to perceive the sublimity of the most simple, ordinary things.

'Good snowflakes – they don't fall anywhere else.' A single snowflake is just as sublime as the Milky Way. There's something about stilling and sharpening attention that allows an intimacy with the ordinary that reveals how extraordinary ordinary things are.

One of the most precise definitions of Sŏn meditation is found in a letter written by Keats to his brothers Thomas and George in December 1817, where he explores his idea of 'negative capability'. This is what we're doing here: we're cultivating negative capability. And how did Keats define it? He said:

> *That is when a man is capable of resting in mysteries, uncertainties and doubts without any irritable reaching after fact or reason.*[21]

Keats knew nothing at all about Buddhism, let alone Sŏn – it wasn't that he ignored them; there was simply no information available on either at that time. But his definition of negative capability describes the practice of 'What is this?' as well as, if not better than, much of what you'll find in the Sŏn texts themselves. Perhaps the only word that doesn't quite ring true is 'irritable', which would suggest to a contemporary person something like 'slightly pissed off'. But we need to remember that Keats trained at Guy's Hospital to be a surgeon and was qualified as an apothecary. In the early nineteenth century, 'irritable' – in the context of medicine – meant 'reflexive'. In other words, a leg was 'irritable' if you tapped it on the knee and it made a reflexive jerk. It had nothing to do with being annoyed or angry.

So 'without any *irritable* reaching after fact or reason' means without any automatic, reflexive, reactive reaching after fact or reason. In that sense it's very close to what happens when we ask 'What is this?'. There we are, sitting on a cushion, trying to 'rest in mysteries, uncertainties and doubts' – only for the mind to 'irritably' – that is, reactively – clutch on to an idea, a story or some rational answer to the question, which sends us off into la-la land again.

Sometimes when asking this question, you might find it rather uncomfortable and unsettling. This can happen even, or perhaps especially, when you become fully engaged with it. All of a sudden, the question shifts into another register, as it were, and you find yourself exposed to the enormity of what you simply don't know. This can be scary. It upsets our convictions about who we are, what the world is. So in order not to get drawn any further into this unstructured openness, the mind latches on to a familiar and comforting idea. You might, for example, think you've come up with the 'answer' – a suitably enigmatic and zenny answer, of course – or else you get carried away by an idea, a theory, a story, which is so much easier to live with than sustaining this disquieting sense of perplexity and ignorance.

I'm going to end here. I hope what I've said might help you find a way to engage with this practice that makes it more than just a form of Buddhist meditation from the far east. I hope it provides you with some tools not just for reflecting on classical kongans but for confronting the kongan of your own life, as well as the kongan of this universe – that we fleetingly inhabit.

Wednesday morning

I don't know

Stephen Batchelor

Let's start with another passage from a letter by John Keats. On 27 January, 1818, Keats attended a lecture by the critic William Hazlitt entitled 'On Shakespeare and Milton'. He was particularly struck by how Hazlitt described Shakespeare as:

> *The least of an egotist that it was possible to be. He was nothing in himself, but he was all that others were or that they could become.* [22]

This, I think, is entirely relevant to the practice of 'What is this?'. Rather than address the act of questioning itself, Keats's remark considers its flip side: unknowing. Unknowing is a necessary condition for the emergence of any fresh insight or understanding. For as long as we're convinced about something, it is very difficult to see it in another way. Unknowing also has to do with the opening up of the imagination, as well as the capacity to empathise with others.

It allows us to see, think and act differently. I have already suggested that how you respond to 'What is this?' may not express itself in words at all. A more appropriate response to the question might take the form of a painting, a poem or some other work of art, which originates not in our cognitive faculties but in being liberated to form a picture or image or sound, in which an insight is shown or displayed rather than uttered as a truth claim.

Many of the stories we hear in Sŏn point in this direction. They insist that we put aside any notion of coming up with the 'right' answer to the *kongan*, one which accords with Buddhist or Sŏn doctrine. No. It's about experiencing life in a way that's unconstrained by the limits of what can be said, but can still be imagined. In another letter, also written in 1818, Keats expands on this idea and says:

> As to the poetical Character itself ... it is not itself – it has no
> self – It is everything and nothing – It has no character – it
> enjoys light and shade; it lives in gusto, be it foul or fair, high
> or low, rich or poor, mean or elevated – It has as much delight
> in conceiving an Iago as an Imogen. What shocks the virtuous
> philosopher delights the chameleon poet.[23]

Scholars and priests of Buddhist orthodoxy often find the ways in which Sŏn teachings are presented as shocking. 'You can't say that!' they say, thus revealing how the creeping momentum of doctrinal correctness and ecclesiastical authority so often ends up with dry, complicated dogmas, thereby losing touch with the sources of the creative imagination that generate metaphors, imagery and poems.

We see this very clearly in the history of Indian Buddhism. What's striking in many of the early discourses is Gotama's love of metaphor and concrete images as a means to illustrate his teaching. Consider the water imagery, for example, that you find throughout the Pali canon: how the eightfold path is compared to a stream, how reactivity is described as arid, how the practitioner should be like a farmer irrigating a field, how Māra (or Namuci) 'holds back the waters', and so on. The Buddha likewise uses many examples drawn from his observations of the work of artisans. In the *Satipaṭṭhāna sutta*, for instance, you have him comparing someone who is mindful of their breath to a skilled woodturner working with a lathe or an expert butcher cutting up the carcass of a cow.

All this points away from the sort of knowledge privileged by scholars, who claim to know what is the nature of truth or reality, towards the hands-on expertise or know-how of the carpenter, the farmer, the goldsmith, the surgeon. Whether deliberately or not, Sŏn picks up and recovers that current of thinking, which became marginalised, even forgotten, as the tradition was increasingly dominated by abstract thinking. And I don't think it's accidental that of all the Buddhist traditions alive today, it's only in Sŏn that you find a complete integration of the arts into dharma practice. Calligraphy, brush painting, poetry, gardening, tea drinking: all these are considered as valid forms of practice in their own right, not merely as adjuncts to meditation. 'The taste of tea and the taste of Sŏn are one' is a phrase I heard many times in Korea. At the same time, in Sŏn monasteries the monks are expected to till the fields, harvest the crops, prepare kimchi for winter, dredge the river, or get involved in whatever work needs to be done. 'A day without work is a day without food' is another commonly-cited aphorism. There's a hands-on engagement with the world that draws upon a know-how, on skills that are enacted with the muscles and nerves of the body, thereby no longer reducing knowledge to what can be achieved by the mind alone.

Anyway, let's get back to how these ideas might be put into practice on this retreat. I want to talk about the flip side of questioning, what I have already referred to as unknowing. If you're familiar with Sŏn writings, this is an idea that is traditionally expressed in terms like 'no-mind' or 'no-thought'. I like unknowing because it suggests something more processual, something we can cultivate and develop over time, rather than simply to aim at the absence of thought or mental activity, which can easily be misconstrued as a blank-minded quietism.

Unknowing is implicit in any act of questioning. For you can only ask a question with sincerity if you actually don't know something. It's only when you don't know, for example, where Newton Abbot is in relation to Gaia House, that can you ask in good faith, 'Where is Newton Abbot?'. In uttering that question, you tacitly affirm, 'I don't know where Newton Abbot is'. We sometimes forget this. So what can help here in asking the question: 'What is this?' is periodically to say to ourselves with just as much emphasis, 'I don't know what this is. I really don't know.'.

The Korean Sŏn teacher Seung Sahn coined a phrase that's become popular among meditators: *don't know mind*. He would say in his emphatic but broken English: 'Only don't know mind!'.[24] This, I feel, is a crucial dimension of the practice. So today, every now and again replace 'What is this?' with 'I don't know'. Instead of resting in the pregnant silence that follows from asking 'What is this?' now let yourself feel in the body what happens after saying, 'I don't know what this is', or simply 'I don't know'. As with asking the question, just let yourself rest in the wordless aftermath of that pronouncement, sensing in your flesh and bones what it's like not to know, to be bewildered, confused, unknowing.

Now, we live in a society, and I suspect most societies have been like this, where we privilege knowledge over ignorance, knowing over unknowing. As for myself, in many social situations I feel an almost physical urge welling up inside to be the one who knows. If I'm involved in a discussion, particularly if it concerns Buddhism – about which I like to think of myself as an 'expert' – I notice that there's a part of me that is so emotionally invested in being the one who knows about this subject, that I get more than a little bit irked if somebody doesn't seem to properly respect my authority.

This common human experience shows how very concerned we are to be 'in the know'. What we know gives us a sense of validation, legitimacy, and self-confirmation, whereas feelings of unknowing, uncertainty and doubt can be deeply unsettling. Such feelings expose cracks and fissures in the solid wall of our certainties and reveal how we are prone to error. I feel this particularly strongly when someone points out a mistake in what I have published. This takes the wind out of my sails, I feel myself sinking into an abyss of foolishness.

I was recently taken to task about my translation of a passage in the *Ariyapariyesana sutta* – the *Discourse on the noble quest*.[25] Having read the criticism, I had to accept that my critic's knowledge of Pali was far greater than mine, and he was probably right in what he said. But I didn't take what he said as a neutral piece of information: 'Oh, that's interesting. I won't make that mistake again.' His words were like a knife to the belly, which for days left a knotted wound of discomfort inside me. These moments are very helpful, because they expose the extent to which the ego is invested in being right, in being able to strut about with confidence and certainty in the correctness of one's views and opinions. Yet the practice of 'What is this?' – indeed any practice that is concerned with getting to the core of what it means to be fully human – has to risk being open to the uncomfortable fact that we are vastly ignorant of what is going on.

Take the simple example of the human ability to perceive light. Our eyes have evolved to see only a tiny range of light rays within the overall spectrum of what is potentially visible. We are ignorant of the rest of the spectrum not because we are stupid but because we are human beings. It is simply impossible to register these rays of light with the unaided human eye. In the western philosophical tradition, of course, we find this point elaborated much further by Immanuel Kant. Kant recognised how the extent of possible human knowledge is constrained by the structure of our body and mind. This means that we are incapable of knowing more than just a minute percentage of what actually constitutes reality. Yet we suffer the conceit of thinking that we are terribly smart beings who have pretty much got reality sorted out and cracked. In the example I gave yesterday about the Big Bang: it's extremely difficult for us even to think of something that could not happen in time or space, which, for Kant, are understood as *categories of apperception*. Time and space are like a fisherman's net. What we can know unaided is limited to those things that are the right 'size' and 'shape' to be 'caught' in that net. Only then can we say that we are 'conscious' of something. The rest is simply beyond our possible comprehension – like the rays of light outside the range of what our eyes can see.

In the same way, my two cats at home will never understand differential calculus. Let alone mathematics, my cats can't even figure out that it's a bad idea to walk through any door that happens to be left ajar. Cats cannot understand that a door in a house inhabited by humans is likely to be closed afterwards and they will get locked in. I learn a lot from observing my cats. It is very clear that a cat is innocently enveloped in an ignorance that it cannot possibly override. I can never teach my cats certain things – like the dangers of going through an open door. It's just not going to happen. And that's not because the cat is stupid, it's because the cat's a cat.

It's the same with us. Simply because we're human there are certain things that we just aren't going to know. It's not because we are stupid. It's simply the way we are built. This, to me, suggests the need for humility. To acknowledge and cultivate unknowing and questioning is very much about being open to the fact that the world is profoundly mysterious and strange. But that's something that our ego resists and ignores. I suspect this habit must have conferred survival advantages in our ancestral past. After all, it's not much help in the struggle for survival on the African savannah to sit cross-legged on the ground and declare to one's fellow tribe members, 'Shit, this is weird – I haven't got a clue who I am or what's happening'. Such a person is far less likely to survive in that environment to pass on their genetic material – the fertile young women of the tribe would be unlikely to be drawn to you as a mate who could reliably provide for them and their offspring. It's far more advantageous to be able to say, 'Look, I know where the food is and where the dangers are, and right now the enemy is hiding behind that hill, but he doesn't know that I know that, so we can easily ambush and kill him before he launches his raid to steal the deer that we just hunted'. That's the kind of knowledge that will impress the girls and afford you and them survival advantages.

One of the privileges of living in a relatively safe and prosperous world is to have the education and leisure to be able to ask these kinds of questions. We are free to make use of our consciousness – even though it may have evolved for very different reasons – to open ourselves to the fact that we don't know. In Sŏn, this unknowing is not regarded as a failing or a weakness; rather the opposite. It's what allows us to be more honest, more truthful, and – to some extent – more humble. It allows the world to be disclosed to us in a way that's not narrowly defined by how much knowledge I have about it and how great an expert I am on this that and the other.

This is a kind of agnosticism. The very word agnostic means not-knowing. But here we have a *deep* agnosticism, which is very similar to Keats's negative capability: when one can 'be with mysteries, uncertainties and doubts without any irritable reaching after fact and reason', the quality that 'Shakespeare possessed so enormously'. This wasn't a weakness or a failure on Shakespeare's part; it was his greatest gift. Because when we come to rest in that wondering openness of unknowing and questioning, we are liberated from the constraints of our knowledge, certainties and convictions, which so often have the consequence of narrowing and dulling our lives.

In other words, such convictions can function as anaesthetics. I'm taking that word very literally: 'an-aesthetic'. Rather than enhancing our aesthetic appreciation of the world, our knowledge and certainties function as anaesthetics. They dull us, they numb us. They might, of course, give us advantages in our work and career, but – as a side effect – they are an-aesthetic.

They render the rest of the world flat, opaque, uninteresting, boring. One of the really central aspects of mindfulness or Sŏn practice – or any kind of comparable discipline – is that its purpose is not to grant us further knowledge. That's a rather dangerous track to go down: to seek more knowledge, better knowledge, 'ultimate' knowledge. Be careful.

This practice, I've found, opens up our capacity for a deeper aesthetic experience of life, what I spoke of earlier as the 'sublime'. This way of being in the world may not provide us with the comforts of certitude, but rather the overwhelming sense of being a relatively insignificant part of something that infinitely outstrips our capacity for representation. Therein, I feel, lie the sources of imagination, of creativity, of spontaneity, and – as we'll see in the talk tomorrow evening – of empathy and our capacity for ethical intuitions.

What I'd like you to do today is to try to come back every now and again to 'I don't know' and let that percolate into your nervous system so that you feel it in the torso, you feel it in your arms and legs, as a felt-sense rather than a concept. And just see where that takes you.

Wednesday evening

Emptiness

Martine Batchelor

This evening I'd like to talk about emptiness. This subject features prominently in the Korean Sŏn tradition, and there are various ways to approach it.

One of the main, frequently chanted texts in the Korean Sŏn tradition comes from the Mahayana tradition. Very likely it's a shortened version of the *Heart sutra* that might have arisen in China, received wide acceptance, and in this way has become part of the tradition. Some of you might already know it.

One of its well-known lines lays down that 'form is emptiness, emptiness is form'. What does this mean? That all forms are empty? Does it mean that emptiness does not exist? If all forms are empty, does this mean that everything is empty? But if we go on to say, 'emptiness is form', then emptiness does not exist either! So what is being talked about here? What is this concept of emptiness about? We need to clear this up, because the concept of emptiness often becomes reified, such that we get the impression that there must be some mystical 'emptiness' somewhere that we need to experience.

In another other part of the *Heart sutra* we read, 'For this reason, in emptiness there is no form; no feeling; no perception, impulse, consciousness; no eyes, ears, nose, tongue, body, mind.' The Sŏn tradition bases itself on this concept of emptiness, which it views differently from the early tradition. The concept already occurs in the early tradition, but in a developmental stage. The same wording appears in one of the early teachings, the *Kassaka sutta*,[26] where the Buddha says, 'Where no eye exists, no forms exist, no sphere of consciousness and contact at the eyes exists'. Here we find the same negations: no eyes, no ears, no contact.

But then the Buddha concludes the discourse by saying, 'What they speak of is not mine'. This might give us a clue about what emptiness is about. It's not some kind of mystical emptiness, but is more about non-identification.

Nāgārjuna is one of the great elucidators of emptiness in the wider Buddhist tradition. He was a significant Mahayana philosopher whom many Buddhist traditions honour to this day. Here is what he says about emptiness, as Stephen translates him:

> *Buddhas say emptiness is relinquishing opinions. Believers in emptiness are incurable.*

Nāgārjuna asks, 'What does it mean to be empty?'. For him emptiness means that nothing exists independently of what forms it. Instead of positing a mystical emptiness that we need to discover, he's talking about empty*ing*. What we are left with, then, is not nothing, but rather what I call *creative engagement.*

The image that comes to me is the washer-uppers. We have four plastic buckets full of cups, bowls and plates. Though everybody here is trying to be good and eat up everything on their plate, there's still a little food encrusted on them. If we didn't have the washer-uppers who wash the plates and put them back clean, would we want to still use them? The plate wouldn't be not-empty if it wasn't washed. Let's consider a single plate: there isn't much on it, but there's still something – a residue which hasn't been washed away. But when the kind washer-uppers clean all the plates, bowls, and cups, then they're all empty. And because they're empty of any residue, then we can fill that emptiness with something else. We can pour tea into them, ladle soup into them, and dish out solid food onto them.

I hope this shows how the idea of emptiness captures the dynamic process of life itself, of our organism itself. On one side you have the emptying, and on the other side of that emptying you have the creative engagement.

This is what I want to draw attention to: what it is we're emptying on a retreat. As we sit in meditation, we have thoughts, sensations and emotions, and we hear sounds. We might think, 'Well, this isn't empty! I'm feeling a sensation! I'm experiencing an emotion! I'm having a thought! I'm hearing a sound!' I mean, we heard the 'boinggggg' of the door when it fell to the floor – something definitely happened. So it wasn't empty.

However, it is *empty of self-existence.* The movement and noise resulting from the falling of the door depended on many different things, such as the weakness of the hinges, and something else must have happened to finish it off. We have so many different experiences on a retreat. It's an opportunity to cultivate emptying, to experience it, but also to experience and understand the opposite movement – of grasping, of identifying. It's also an opportunity to check out, 'How does it happen?'. To me that is what is so fascinating: seeing clearly that part of the process.

The Japanese Zen master Dōgen said, 'The way of the Buddha is to know the self. To know the self is to forget the self. To forget the self is to be enlightened by all things.' Thus before the emptying comes the task of knowing ourselves. So our questioning and self-awareness homes in on inquiries such as, 'How do I grasp? And what happens when I grasp?' While noting, with the Buddha, that it doesn't belong to 'me'.

We are this organism which encounters the world. We come into contact with inner conditions and outer conditions. Again and again, we seem to do two things. One is to say 'This is me! This condition is me!'. Or we grasp at – and identify with – a condition, and then proliferate around it. The emptying process doesn't lead us to say, 'Nothing exists'! Rather leads us to the insight that, 'Things exist, there is function, there is process, but do I need to identify with it in a certain way?'.

The question arises because it seems to be 'me' who experiences it. Nobody else is experiencing the pain in my back; nobody else is experiencing my thought, nobody else is experiencing my emotions, so at that level it is 'me' who is experiencing it, and not somebody else. But *how* am 'I' experiencing it? Do I need to grasp and identify with these experiences? On retreat, with heightened awareness, we can opt for an alternative, and see how emptying leads to an openness, so the creative potential can arise in the experience, and creatively engaging becomes possible. Grasping and identifying stop that creative process in its tracks.

There are a few new people here this evening, so I'll do my party trick. I know many of you might have seen it, but this performance is for the ones who haven't seen it before. Let's say this object I'm holding is special. Indeed it's actually very special to Stephen, who wanted me to put it in the luggage because he loves it. Let's say it's special to me too. Because it's special to me, it belongs to me, so then I grasp at it. If I grasp it for any length of time, two things are going to happen. The first is that I'm going to get a cramp in the arm, and generally this tension is a sign of grasping.

Secondly, if I grasp the object in this way, I can't use my hand for anything else, so I'm stuck to what I'm grasping. It's really vital to realise this point. The process of emptying comes down to slowly ungrasping, releasing our hold so we can move again. The object still exists, I can still use it, but the tightness is gone. With grasping comes identifying – the two go together. I, me, mine – the convergence is very strong: grasping and identifying go together.

That's why, when we talk of emptying, we're talking about not-self. As the Buddha says, 'it doesn't belong to me'. But that doesn't mean I can't experience the object in question, that I can't use it. On the other hand, if we grasp then we identify, and in this way we limit ourselves to what we identify with. And our next move is even more problematic: we *amplify* around it. This is something we can notice – how quickly we can either proliferate around something or exaggerate. If we ever say the words 'always' or 'never', we know we're grasping and identifying, because we're exaggerating.

We grasp in different ways. We can grasp as in 'I want this', and you amplify around that. I love to shop in Oxford Street once or twice a year. When I last visited Oxford Street, what did I buy? I spent an hour and a half walking from Oxford Circus to Marble Arch, and I bought a pair of socks and some salt which actually comes from France but I can only buy it in England! Why did I buy it? Because I needed it, and I could not find anything else I needed. It's very interesting when you look through the shop window and think, 'do I need this?'.

When we grasp at something, we can easily proliferate or

exaggerate: 'I have to have this! If I *have* this my life will be transformed!'. To follow the ancient adage, 'Know thyself' in this situation is to ask, 'Oooh, am I proliferating here?'. That would mean
I'm grasping, I'm identifying. 'Am I exaggerating here?' would be
another pertinent question. The same sequence can unfold in a
negative way, starting with 'I hate this'. In both cases we're amplifying.

So what constitutes a self? When this kind of questioning
of self – thinking of emptying of self – occurs, two different aspects
come into play. One aspect is the impression that there *is* a self,
that there is something which is 'me', and the way we can notice
it is in feeling self-conscious. Next, we can question this kind of
feeling of self when we hear somebody say something to us. They
might say something unpleasant, or they might have said something unpleasant to us perhaps five or ten years ago, and we still
remember it.

Years later we're sitting here in silent retreat, and the unpleasant word is still coming up! So there must be a self somewhere
to whom the unpleasant word is going to stick, right? Often we
can get the impression that something like a pin cushion sits in
the middle of the body, and whenever somebody says something
unpleasant or hurtful... 'ping!'. It's like there's a new pin plunging
in, and from time to time you inadvertently move it so a drop of
blood comes out. 'Ooh, that was painful!'. But there isn't any pin
cushion! There's no bodily cavity into which the pin can enter!
This is what's so interesting about words. They're empty because
they're just sonorous waves, yet we hear a word and then stick it
somewhere. Where? Can't we just leave it to arise, consider it, ask
if it says anything about me (or not), and then just let it be?

We can follow suit with various other inner conditions.
When we ask, 'Am I grasping?' and the answer seems to me no,
what might be an alternative way to identify? We can grasp at some-

thing as if it belongs to us, even though it's just a condition arising, which will pass away. For example, a thought. What is a thought? I know we've had lots of thoughts (even if I hope you have less thoughts as the day goes by), but what are thoughts, really? They're just a little electricity in the brain. Is electricity 'me'? Am I defining myself by little electrical charges in my brain, saying, 'This is me'? Or is it just a little electricity arising; I can cling to it, or not. And if I don't cling to it, then – poof! – like everything else it'll pass.

Or are we identifying with – grasping at – sensation? Sensations seem more palpable, so okay, they're really there; that must mean that they exist, and hence so do 'I'. Sensation… that must be me. But you don't have them all the time, you have them only from time to time. In the Sŏn tradition, they don't practise 'body scanning'. When Stephen and I put together a book of our teacher Master Kusan's teachings, we asked him for a little story about his life. He said, 'Alright, I'll tell you a few stories'. Teachers don't usually do that, but he was kind enough to do so.

He told us a wonderful story about a time when he had a meeting with a distant friend, so he had to walk very fast for many hours. There were few means of transport in those days, so he had to walk far and fast to meet his friend. When he arrived he suddenly felt really, really ill. So he lay down and thought, 'Pfff! I'm really in bad shape' – identifying with, grasping at the sensations. But then he thought, 'Wait a minute! Where can I find this pain? Where is it, this pain?' And he did a body scan, he looked through the whole body bit by bit, and concluded that he couldn't find the pain anywhere, whereupon he felt much better!

Personally, I think he initially grasped at and identified with the pain, which added what the Buddha called 'the second arrow': he was so worried about it that it became exaggerated. Through the questioning – 'What is this? Where can I find it?' – he then came back to what was going on

So do we identify with our sensations, perhaps even with an illness? Do we define ourselves by it? Or do we *creatively engage* with it?

Many years ago I was on a one-month silent retreat. It was a great opportunity to do a month-long retreat and no teaching, just sitting there. So I was really keen. We could get up at four o'clock in the morning and sit all day. But on the second day I was ill with a gastric condition, which happens sometimes, and I was aware I that had 28 more days on retreat. I realised that if I grasped: 'I have this pain in the stomach, this is terrible, how am I going to sit with this for 28 days?', then the retreat would become impossible. Instead I chose to creatively engage, and asked, 'When is the pain happening? How long does it last? What is it that helps it to change?'

I'd sit in meditation and observe how the pain was there one minute, then it wasn't there the next minute. Then it might come back, then it might go again. I noticed that if I lay down it was better; if I went for walks it was better; and in this way I was able to take advantage of those 28 days on retreat. By creatively engaging I could still experience some pain, but not reduce myself to it. This is one of the problems with grasping, with identifying: we reduce ourselves to just one of the conditions that form us. We can also reduce ourselves to one emotion – be that sadness, anger, or fear. And fear can be so paralysing. After all, fear is a survival mechanism, a human emotional function.

When I was living in Korea, we decided to do a non-sleep week, which means you sit in meditation all the time, day and night. I didn't worry about the sitting. I was actually worrying about going to the bathroom at night. It was outside, and at one o'clock in the morning it's dark out there. I thought, 'Ooh, I'm going to have a heart attack if I go out there'. I used to be very afraid of the dark. So I went to Master Kusan and asked, 'Master, what can I do? I'm afraid of the dark'. He said 'Ask the question: what is this?'. I thought, 'Okay, it's like magic, it's going to save me from the bad guys out there'. So at one o'clock in the morning I'd go out and say 'What is this? What is this? What is this? What is this?...'. It worked!

I realised that before, when I'd go out, I had this premonition, 'There's a guy with a knife, he's going to get me! Ahhh!'. But now, when I asked, 'What is this? What is this? What is this?', I suddenly realised, 'Who is going to know I'm here and come and get me in the middle of nowhere in Korea?'. De-exaggeration, de-proliferation arises from realising that emptying doesn't mean not having a thought, a sensation, an emotion. It means that we don't grasp at it, we don't identify with it. This is what emptying is about.

When we mention emptiness, people often say, 'Oh! Everything is empty... I must be empty... so then I cannot love.'. Someone actually said to me once, 'I can't drink coffee. I can't love coffee if everything is empty'. I thought that was going a little far. But if we mustn't grasp, if everything is empty, then how can I love somebody? That's not what emptiness is about. If we don't grasp at ourselves, if we don't grasp at the other, then – on the contrary – we'll have what I call creative, wise love. When you fall in love with somebody, or when you love your children or your friends or your cat or whatever it might be, you feel warmer and lighter. That's a very significant quality. Lovingkindness practice nurtures this formative experience of warmth and lightness.

Before my grandmother died two years ago, she suddenly lost a certain level of connection. It was enormously sad. Before that, she was so happy to see me. Then something changed; she'd see me but there was no longer any warmth. The lightness she'd feel when she saw me had gone, but she still experienced it with flowers. So she'd go into the garden, where she'd cut huge branches with lots of blooms, and she'd bring them to us. I felt this was a way she could connect to the warmth and lightness. Or when there were animals present, for instance when my niece brought a little bunny, she'd stay next to it, because for a few moments it let her feel the warmth and lightness anew. This is what love is about – loving another, loving ourselves.

Often we don't like ourselves. This is a bit self-defeating, because we're stuck with ourselves all the time, even if we don't like ourselves! It's unpleasant to be stuck with somebody we don't like. But if we love ourselves, we'll be warm all the time! This is an easy way to be warm and light; and if we love others, this adds to the experience. But when we love others, what is it we grasp at? Do we grasp at the person, which means that we want to be with her or him all the time? Do we grasp at the feeling the other is giving us? And if the feeling isn't always there, does that mean we don't love the other person? So when we love somebody, what is actually going on? Are we grasping at the other person? Are we grasping at the feeling? Or are we caring, and appreciating having her/him in our life? One of the most beautiful things we can do is to love some-one, and to be loved, because basically you're saying to the other person, 'I see you, I know you, I accept you'. This is a tremendous gift to give others, and to experience oneself.

Can we bring this creative engagement – this wise creative love – to all our relationships, including to our children? In the children's case, do we love the child as s/he appears, or do we love the *idea* of the child? I had a friend who absolutely wanted a child, but his wife wasn't keen on having a child. She said, 'Alright, if you really want a child, then these are my conditions. Every year, for one month, I go on retreat on my own and you'll take care of the child.'. He signed up to her conditions. He told me all the reasons he wanted a child, and I silently hoped that he wasn't going to put all his expectations onto the child. He seemed to be grasping at that child, what the child would bring into his life.

Fortunately he's also a meditator and a teacher. Thus when the child arrived, everything changed. He creatively engaged with the new human being, who had certain qualities, who was connected to her father but was also developing along her own lines. The *emptying* in terms of relationships is not about pushing the other person away – 'I must not be attached!'. Rather, it's about asking oneself, 'Can I meet this other person for himself or herself?'. This is creative, wise love: to really see the person for themselves, and not for myself; but of course also to appreciate the way in which the sharing, connecting and mutual influencing contribute to my life.

I want to conclude with this thought about emptying. It can be quite a challenge. Even wonderful dharma teachers come up against their limits in this area, I've noticed. They can teach and practise emptiness of eyes, ears and other things that the sutra lists, but there's one kind of emptiness that often eludes them. I find this puzzling. In most traditions, most – though not all – teachers are rather dogmatic about what they teach. They're grasping at the idea that 'my' tradition, 'my' approach to meditation, 'my' technique is right for me – in which case it's the right one, the only one, for everybody. My teacher, Master Kusan, was so adamant about this, that the question *imoko?* – the *hwadu* – was it! Anything else? Forget it!

On one occasion Master Kusan became a footnote in the history of the Insight Meditation Society in Massachusetts, where Joseph Goldstein and Sharon Salzberg teach. It's a large meditation centre in America. In the early days, before they learned better, they used to invite teachers from other traditions. If a great master came by, they would invite her or him to give a talk. In this way Master Kusan came during their three-month silent winter retreat. Unfortunately Master Kusan's translator was, like him, rather dogmatic. All the people gathered had been watching the breath, watching the body, cultivating mindfulness for a month and suddenly this man turns up, exuding authority, and saying, 'Watching the breath! What's the point? This is no better than being a corpse! Forget it! If you want to awaken, ask the question: "What is this?".'

He was never invited back. In fact, they never invited in any other outside teachers again, and for a week Joseph and Sharon were busy taking care of their perplexed and worried meditators. At one level the episode could have been useful in prompting the meditators to ask, 'Should I follow this practice or not? Is this really useful or not?'. I have seen this dogmatism in other teachers – in the Dalai Lama, in Thich Nhat Hanh – who are really great, open-minded teachers, but dogma is their last frontier that doesn't seem empty and connected to conditions.

Since dogmatism tends to be the last frontier of emptiness, we need to take care. We can access our own experience only, and no-one else's. If throughout our meditative lives we've asked, 'What is this?' and we've found that it works, then it's a good method. On the other hand, if we've watched the breath (or noted thoughts) all that time and it's worked, then they're effective methods too. Each of them can further our dharma practice.

I realised this a few years back in the company of a friend, Leigh Brasington, who teaches jhāna retreats that are based on meditative absorption/concentration. We're both really open, trying our best not to be dogmatic. Over two days we talk about everything under the sun, including jhāna and how it works. In the end neither he nor I can say whether his method or mine is better; we can barely admit that our several methods are equally valid. And I could see why: I haven't experienced his method in the way he has, and he hasn't experienced mine in the way I have.

This is something we all need to understand. Some methods will work for us better than others; a particular method might fit about sixty per cent of the people, another around forty per cent, still others a lesser proportion. I know people for whom the breath isn't a good idea; I know others for whom the questioning isn't a good idea. For some people even loving kindness isn't a good idea. But it doesn't mean they can't meditate using another method. This is important to understand, so as to bring about emptying in the method we use, and to ensure that we hold it lightly – not least when we hear the teacher say, 'this is the one true way'.

I'll finish with a poem from one of my favourite nuns in Korea – one who's since died, as she was quite ancient when I met her. I wrote her biography, which contains some of her poems.

> *Empty is the original mind of sentient creatures.*
> *Insubstantial is their being.*
> *Where could a Buddha be born?*
> *Following the way, they rise to Buddhahood.*
> *Committing a crime, they fall into hell.*
> *What futile information!*

Thursday morning

Courage and questioning

Martine Batchelor

Korean Sŏn holds out three great qualities as essential: great faith, great courage, and great questioning. Let's look at them in connection to our practice.

Great faith

'Faith' here doesn't refer to belief in something outside of ourselves, but rather having great confidence in our own potential. It has various facets. For example, at the beginning of a retreat we're trying to convince ourselves this is a good idea: 'Yes, let's do it! My friend thinks it's great, I think it's great, the text says it's great.' This is what I call 'building ourselves up' faith. I noticed it in Korea, when we used to sit for three months; during the first two weeks I'd tell myself: 'I can do it! This is tough. But it's okay. Yes, I can do this!'

For two weeks the body and the mind struggle to get into the rhythm of it. Then after those first two weeks it feels like: 'This is fantastic! I want to do this my whole life!'. And then I don't *need* great faith because I *experience* for myself, and know that experience for what it is. 'Oh yeah! This works, I can do it!'. But then at the end of the retreat, in the last two weeks, for some strange reason I'm ready to leave.

On the present retreat, we're experiencing the same pattern in an abbreviated version. The first two days we think, 'What am I doing here?'. And we try to convince ourselves it's okay. Then hopefully in the middle we think, 'Oh yeah, I know this practice'. And then the great faith is not so much about convincing ourselves, but about experiencing: 'Oh yeah, I have this potential, I can do this practice'. And then in the last days the great faith might change again: 'I can do this practice here, but how am I going to follow it in my daily life?'. We'll talk more about that on Friday and Saturday.

Great faith takes different forms. Sometimes we're convincing ourselves, reminding ourselves, pumping ourselves up. At other times we're just experiencing it. At still other times we need to remember that great faith exists, even if we're not experiencing it just then. So far we've been lucky: a week ago we heard it was going to rain every day, but it held off until last night. So the sun has cheered us on. Every day when the sun shines when you're in England in April, it's like 'Wow, this is great!'. Now we have clouds for company. We're not experiencing the sun any more, but we know it still exists, it's still there, above the clouds. Similarly we need to know, during our practice on retreat, that great faith is still there, even though the practice might be really difficult right now. The potential is still there, the experience can come back. Great faith gives us a ground, an underpinning for our practice.

Great courage

Great courage means putting out energy for the practice, giving it oomph. But often we think of it more as an heroic courage. We might vow to sit nonstop! For myself, I think great courage actually refers to going beyond our habits, going a little beyond our limits. It's having the courage to creatively engage, to make the choice to come back. It's the courage to be present for the whole experience. And to question.

Here is a quote from the sixth patriarch whom Stephen mentioned earlier:

> *No-thought is to see and to know all things with a mind free from grasping.*

'No-thought' doesn't mean having no thoughts at all. Rather, it's to see and know all things with a mind free from grasping. He goes on:

> *When in use it pervades everywhere and yet it sticks nowhere.*

No-thought means having the great courage not to get stuck, because we stick so easily.

> *What we have to do is to purify our mind...*

Personally I'd rather translate this line as 'What we have to do is creatively engage...'

> *...so that the six aspects of consciousness, in passing through the six sense organs, will be neither influenced nor attached to the six sense objects.*

Could we play with that idea in terms of great courage to-day? I come into contact with a thought; I come into contact with a feeling, a sensation, a sound. Can I creatively engage with it? Can I have the great courage to avoid immediately sticking to it? And not pushing it away in aversion (which would amplify it). Can we have the great courage to creatively engage, to be really present for what's going on without sticking to it? Can we play around with that today?

We exemplify great courage when we apply ourselves with that effortless effort. And sometimes we express it by accepting our limits. For instance, after sitting for years on the floor to meditate, I found I couldn't do it any more, so I had to exert great courage to sit on a chair. That was okay. On occasion it can require great courage to just wholeheartedly apply the practice.

I cooperate in a French research project into meditation. Recently I went through an fMRI machine for the first time. People warned me about claustrophobia and the noise involved. But I don't suffer from claustrophobia and don't mind sounds, so I thought, 'Should be a piece of cake!'. I arrive at the laboratory and every-body goes, 'Ah! A meditation teacher. Okay, let's do it'. But as soon as they put a thick foam collar around my neck my whole body and mind protests, because it's pressing down on the windpipe. My whole body says, 'No way! We're not going to do this!'. I start to hyperventilate. 'Uh-uh!', I say to the lab assistant.

We look at each other, both wondering if we're going to scuttle the test before we even start – three full days of this are planned! I think, 'Okay, I can do it. Great courage! I can do this.'. So then we put the collar back on and I lie down, while my body is still protesting, 'Don't do this, it's a bad idea!'. But I summon up great courage, slide into the machine and repeat to myself the mantras, 'I can do it! I can do it! I can do it! What is this? What is this? What is this?'. I focus on the breath, listen to the sound. I did all these together for ten minutes nonstop. After ten minutes I felt like I was in nirvana – it was amazing! As was the rest of the session. But I needed the great courage to persevere, to collect myself in a way which allowed the body to stop amplifying, and then to relax into the situation. Great courage gives us energy, and allows us to explore.

Great questioning

We've talked a lot about questioning, so how do I question? How can I bring questioning into my meditation? We don't usually associate meditation with questioning – people associate it much more with being calm, with anchoring, concentration and focusing. So how do we question in meditation instead? I read an article by a monk about three masters in Korea and the different ways in which they taught. The article has a backstory, as Stephen has pointed out: Chan/Sŏn/Zen arose in China in the eighth century of our era to counteract the over-scholarly nature of Buddhism at the time. But then Chan itself became too scholarly, deploying a repertoire of stories and 'cases' (kōans) in a rarefied poetic manner as a teaching tool.

Then, in the eleventh century, Dahui[27] committed the ultimate Chan crime: he burned the book in which his master had famously collected all the kōans. But it was this same Dahui who developed the method we're practising on this retreat. He took the kernel of the main kōan and turned it into a question. He thought it'd present a more accessible way for ordinary people to practise. He attracted many lay people from the government as his students. He wanted to give them something they could easily use instead of accumulating lots of stories and poems. They would just have to ask 'What is this?' or whatever question he suggested for them.

Hence we have this question: 'What is this?'. How do we work with it? As with any method, there are various ways to apply it. Even in Korea, if we look at just the three teachers in the article, each one approaches it in a different way. The first teacher, Song-dam Sunim, harnesses it to the breath. We breathe in, and as we breathe out we ask, 'What is this?'. But as he teaches it, you first have to master a particular way of breathing. He gets you to count the breaths, and once you've stabilised, you bring in the questioning with the breath. At first you ask, on the out breath, 'What is this?', then every fifth breath on the out breath, 'What is this?' Finally you ask the question on every tenth breath. His idea is to develop *the sensation* of questioning, and then you just have to ask, 'What is this?' once, and it stays with you the whole day.

Another master, Seong-cheol Sunim, warned against adopting the stance of just observing yourself asking the question, and then registering what is going on, and he too underlined the importance of summoning up the actual sensation of questioning. He suggested we add a few words to the question, for instance: 'What is this? It's not the Buddha, it's not the mind, it's not a material thing, then... what is this?'. That's how he thought the practice could intensify the questioning.

The third teacher touched on in the article is Subul Sunim. I'm going to practice with Subul Sunim in June, so we'll see how his method works. It could hardly be more different! 'Forget about calmness, you don't need to be calm – just the question!', he says. We 'question, but find the answer experientially'. How does he do that? I'll see when I get there.

This overview indicates that there's a variety of ways to ask the focal question. With any type of practice – be it questioning, following the breath, lovingkindness, listening – each of us must over time find a way to make it our own. We make it our own by asking ourselves, 'How can I cultivate (and at the same time integrate) anchoring, questioning, and looking deeply?'. All these teachers emphasise that we don't just question when we're sitting, but also in daily life. How can we keep it up throughout the day? When I go to the bathroom: 'what is this?'. When I'm eating: 'what is this?'. When I'm working: 'what is this?'.

On a retreat we have the opportunity to work on that continuity. We sit and we walk in a continuous sequence. When we leave this room we ask ourselves, 'How can I continue with the questioning?'. We can try to continue with the questioning itself: 'What is this?'. When I was in Korea I once decided to help in the kitchen, helping to cook rice for a hundred people. The kitchen has now been modernised, but back then we used a huge cauldron. We had to put big handfuls of twigs and branches on the fire. When we went to put the cooked rice in a big serving pot we actually had to pick up the rice with a spade. We were feeding so many people. I found that asking 'What is this?' gave me a lot of energy. So I asked 'What is this? What is this?' as I performed the tasks, and boosted my energy the whole time.

When we go for a walk, what actually happens when we walk? Often we're thinking of something else. I use walking to ask the question 'What is this?', bringing the question to mind when I walk in nature. The teachers I've mentioned challenge us to maintain the questioning as we work, and drink our tea. We can either revisit the question, or think more about cultivating a certain sense of calmness, a certain sense of alertness. The great questioning is really about balancing these two qualities. My teacher used to refer to these as *song song, jok jok*, which means 'alert alert, calm calm'.

Apart from sitting and walking in meditation, how can we continue to cultivate qualities of quietness and stability? When we sit and walk in formal meditation, we're trying to build a certain ground within ourselves: a ground of calm, a ground of alertness. It becomes a refuge. I think all this informal practice – as we eat, as we work, as we rest – is continuing to build that ground. When I stand in the queue, how can I be present? How can I be calm and stable in this moment? What is it that helps me to be alert, to be fully present to the experience without trying to make anything of it?

This is why I'm attracted to queueing and standing. In France we're often queuing in daily life. I often queue in my small local supermarket. We frequently feel we've joined the wrong queue, the slow one, and so we mentally try to hurry it up, and get a little stressed and impatient. But we could just stand there instead. What is going to help you do that? We can see it as an opportunity to do an informal practice. Right there, standing in the queue. Or when we're talking to somebody, when we're driving – in whatever activity we're engaged in. How can we connect to this quality? How can we cultivate it?

I want to finish with a quote from Dahui. In twelfth century China, Dahui was writing back and forth with one of his followers. He wrote:

> *Your letter informs me that you feel that your root nature is dim and dull...*

Obviously the follower is going about his day, he is trying to meditate and he does not feel very alert, whereas in this practice being alert is really important. And that's why Dahui encourages him:

> *...The one who can recognise dim and dull is definitely not dim and dull.*

Thursday evening

TALK

The four great vows

Stephen Batchelor

Let's begin with a passage from the record of a ninth century Sŏn teacher from China who is known by his posthumous title Deshan:

> *Deshan entered the hall and addressed the monks, saying: 'I don't hold to some view about the ancestors. Here there are no ancestors and no Buddhas. Bodhidharma is just an old stinking foreigner. Shakyamuni is a dried up piece of shit. Manjushri and Samantabhadra are dung carriers. What is known as realising the mystery is nothing but breaking through to grab an ordinary person's life. Enlightenment and nirvana are just donkeys' tethering posts. The twelve divisions of the scriptural canon are devil's texts, just paper for wiping infected skin boils. The four*

fruitions and the virtuous states, original mind and the ten
stages, these are just graveyard-guarding ghosts, they'll never
save you.'[28]

Now this kind of language is not uncommon in the Sŏn tradition. Sŏn teachers have a reputation for speaking in this foul-
mouthed, provocative way. But as soon as we elevate these statements into seminal texts of a revered school – in this case, Sŏn
Buddhism – present them in a scholarly translation in a handsome
book – the one I'm quoting from is Andy Ferguson's *Zen's Chinese*
heritage: the masters and their teachings and it's brought to us by a
reputable Buddhist publisher, Wisdom Publications no less – then
we have effectively domesticated and sanitised them. We may fail
to appreciate the delicious irony of a teaching that denounces the
scriptural canon as devil's texts now being included as part of the
very scriptural canon that it ridicules. It's most unlikely that you
will tear out a page from this book to clean an infected skin boil.
Deshan's challenging, iconoclastic remarks are thereby neutralised.

Imagine that you're invited – or let's say I'm invited (it happens sometimes) – to a Buddhist conference with representatives
from all the different schools: senior Theravadin abbots, eminent
Tibetan lamas, enlightened Zen masters, and so on. What would
be their reaction if in the course of my presentation I were to say to
the worthy assembly, 'You know what: Shakyamuni Buddha is just
a dried up piece of shit'? And if I were to say this in all seriousness,
while looking the great ajahns and rinpoches in the eyes? To put it
mildly this would be considered as, well, *impolite*, if not downright
rude and obnoxious. It's the sort of thing that would risk having
me evicted from the room. Of course, Buddhists tend to be nice,
tolerant people, so they probably wouldn't kick me out. But they
wouldn't invite me back.

I like to think that when Deshan originally spoke these

words he actually meant what he was saying. He was not playing some parlour game where, as a polite ploy or convention, he was expected to trot out these kinds of offensive statements. Yet once the whole thing is framed as 'Sŏn Buddhism', the words are liable to lose whatever shock effect they would have had when they were first uttered. So if we're going to take these words seriously – and I do take them seriously – then we need to accept that they were spoken with complete sincerity, with great passion and conviction. Deshan meant every word he said.

To be true to this tradition, we need to go beyond the surface language that's been domesticated by its elevation to canonical status, and reflect more deeply on what Deshan was getting at. I think it's undeniable that he was struggling to give voice to something he regarded as of the utmost importance. He wasn't playing around. Deshan was committed to a practice that wasn't based on an uncritical reverence for tradition or a body of canonical texts, but a practice that speaks to the very core, the very heart of the living person.

I love the expression in the middle of the passage, 'What is known as *realising the mystery* is nothing but breaking through to grab an ordinary person's life'. Deshan will have nothing to do with the safe, consolatory language in which 'spiritual' teachings are often couched. (With all my talk of 'mystery', perhaps I'm guilty of this as well.) He's wants us to get back to the immediacy of the raw, felt experience of being alive, of just being an ordinary person and what that ordinary person's life is like.

Again, we're not talking in the abstract here, we're talking about you and me. We're talking about what it feels like to be sitting here now – your heart is beating, you are breathing, you're aware of a pain in your lower back, and *that is your life*. This, and nothing else, is what the practice is about. It's about what is happening to you right now: what you are seeing and smelling and tasting and hearing and touching and feeling and thinking – *that* is what these teachings are addressing.

This movement that began in China around the sixth century breaks with the kind of default reverence for the distant past with its impossibly perfect teachers and saints, and comes right back to the pulsing beat of our own blood, the firing of the neurons in our brains, and, very centrally, the sheer poignancy of being a suffering, mortal creature: that underlying disquiet that keeps bubbling up as soon as we realise that things are not how we would like them to be.

Thus are we confronted with the core experience of the *dukkha* of our lives. *Dukkha* does not just mean the overtly painful bits of life. It refers to that poignant, unreliable, tragic dimension of experience, which is perhaps most succinctly captured in the sense of our lives being so fragile and brief. So when we ask, 'What is this?' – that is what we're asking about, nothing else. In other words, how do we come to terms with this condition in which we find ourselves now?

Another passage: 'A monk asked Deshan: "What is enlightenment?" Deshan hit him, and said: "Get out, don't shit here!".' Mr. Ferguson's translation primly says, 'Don't defecate here!' But can you imagine anyone actually speaking like that? It's another example of wanting to sanitise the language. 'A monk asked Deshan: "What is the Buddha?" Deshan replied: "An old Indian beggar".'[29] Again, this constant taking things off their pedestals and returning to the raw, unadorned facts of existence.

So what would a comparable, Deshan-inspired, approach to the Buddha's dharma look like today? What would happen were we to challenge some of the sacred truths of the Buddhist religion in order to recover what might lie at the heart of the dharma? Let's take as an example the venerable doctrine of the Four Noble Truths. As I'm sure everyone in this room is aware, for Buddhists the teaching of the Four Noble Truths is the underlying doctrine on which the dharma is grounded. From these four axiomatic truths, it is claimed, one can extrapolate the entirety of what is understood as 'Buddhism'. But I would question that.

In fact, in my recent books that's exactly what I've been doing. I wouldn't claim to be a latter-day Deshan, but the training that I have had in the dharma has always encouraged me to question what I'm taught, not just to blindly accept it as a revealed truth.

I was initially trained in the Tibetan Geluk tradition, which is quite conservative in many ways, but it constantly emphasises the importance of critical analysis, of not taking teachings at face value, not accepting doctrines just because they are time-honoured Buddhist truths, but to subject them to rational examination through study and debate. As a result, I've spent a great deal of time over the years thinking about the Four Noble Truths.

I'd like to get rid of the Four Noble Truths, to be perfectly honest. Deshan would have denounced them as 'graveyard-guarding ghosts', but I would dismiss them as being no different from the kind of metaphysical truth-claims the Buddha consistently refused to comment upon. They are generalised statements about the nature of reality, which are claimed to be true for all time. Here they are:

> *Existence is suffering.*
> *The origin of suffering is craving.*
> *The ending of suffering is the ending of craving.*
> *The path that leads to the ending of suffering is the noble*
>   *eightfold path.*

All four are propositional truth-claims. Buddhists believe that each of these statements directly corresponds to a state of affairs in the world. They are attempts to pin down once and for all the nature of 'reality'. 'What's wrong with that?' you might ask. 'Not only are they reasonable claims that require no belief in anything supernatural, they seem to be borne out by experience.' Such objections show how we tend to take this way of speaking about 'truth' for granted and find it quite natural to think like this. But the way we have come to think of 'truth' is deeply problematic. And it's not just me who says so. From William James to Martin Heidegger, the 'correspondence theory of truth' has been criticised as incoherent. Few philosophers would ascribe to it today. And especially so when we render the term in English with 'T'. Capital 'T' Truth, not just any old truth, but a BIG Truth that lies out there behind the scenes somewhere and *really* matters.

I've found it very liberating to abandon this way of thinking about truth altogether. Instead, I prefer to talk about a set of four noble *tasks*, or *practices*. Now I am well aware that most Buddhist traditions also tend to emphasise the importance of practice. The problem, though, is that by insisting on the language of 'truth' they immediately establish a template for looking at and thinking about these tasks in a particular way. And that way of thinking inevitably gives rise to a kind of discourse that risks taking us off in entirely the wrong direction.

As soon as you say to people – at least those who have not yet been brainwashed by Buddhism – 'Existence is suffering' then, predictably, they'll object, 'But what about all the happiness we experience in life?'. And then you get drawn into this generally fruitless discussion: 'Well, actually what I mean here by suffering is da-da-da-da-da' and off you go! That might be very interesting, but I think it's missing the point.

The point, which is stated explicitly at the conclusion of the Buddha's first discourse, is that each of these 'truths' is something to be acted upon in a specific way. The point of the dharma is not to persuade yourself that existence is suffering, the origin of suffering is craving, and so on, but to *embrace* suffering, to *fully know* it, to come to terms with the life situation that confronts you in this moment. And then to *let go* of the craving, or grasping that arises rather than letting yourself be overwhelmed by it so that it determines how you react to the situation. These are tasks to recognise, perform and master. They're not truth-claims to be accepted or rejected.

As soon as we switch focus in this way – a bit like in a Gestalt switch where you shift from seeing a vase to seeing the profiles of two faces – everything changes. We move from a truth-based metaphysics (which attempts to explain how reality is) to a task-based ethics (which encourages a course of action). And this mirrors exactly the same shift in emphasis that happened when the Sŏn movement began. In other words, what matters is not what you believe but what you say and *do*. Each of these 'truths' is more usefully understood as a task, as something to do with utmost urgency and care. What we're doing on this Sŏn retreat is to practise these four tasks.

The first task requires that we open ourselves whole-heartedly to the condition we find ourselves in right now. And that doesn't mean just your 'inner' experience, what's going on in your mind or what concerns you in your 'spiritual' life. It means this total sense I have of being embedded and embodied in this world with others – not only the others in this room, but the rabbits, birds and insects in the garden, the staff at Gaia House, the neighbours in West Ogwell and, by extrapolation, the entire community and society and biosphere of which we are tacitly – but inevitably – interwoven.

How do we embrace that? How do we say 'yes' to that? The practice of Sŏn is grounded in your ability to say, 'Yes, this is the condition I am in'. The practice of 'What is this?' likewise starts here. Without being able to say 'yes' to all this, how can we genuinely ask what 'this' is? The question sheds further light on who or what we are. It opens up our experience as something ineffable, utterly un-pin-downable. ('To say it is like something,' said Huairang, 'misses the point'.) It reveals how deeply strange, tragic, beautiful, sublime it all is. Yet none of these terms in themselves can capture the totality of what we're experiencing in this moment – in all its complexity, in all its uncanniness, in all its radiance.

To ask 'What is this?' is to practise the first task of embracing *dukkha* – your life – but in such a way that we don't just gaze at it more intensely, but we highlight or distil what is questionable about it. What may have seemed opaque and dull no longer strikes us as uninteresting, but rather as weird and poignant, an object of curiosity and perplexity. 'What is this?' is to ask deeply what it is to be, as T.S. Eliot put it: 'an infinitely gentle, infinitely suffering thing'.[30]

As we do this, we become simultaneously aware of how we are reacting to what we experience. We notice how what bubbles up within us can often be troubling. Maybe it's an aversion or an attraction that triggers an accelerated heart rate, or maybe an anxious narrative that starts chattering away in our heads. As human beings we are reactive creatures. As soon as we encounter a situation, a person, a thing, it is likely to trigger a reaction of some kind. Of course, sometimes that reaction can be a positive one: we respond with kindness, or generosity, or equanimity – just the sort of qualities we seek to cultivate in this practice.

But a crucial point in the Buddha's therapeutic teaching is to focus on those reactions in which we get stuck, that are repetitive and destructive: our attachments, our fears, our jealousies, our pride. These are very deep-seated, at root probably instinctual, but they turn into social and psychological habit patterns that we collectively and individually develop within us over the years. We don't choose them, they just flare up unbidden. Which is perhaps why the Buddha called them 'fires'. And very often they flare up so rapidly and powerfully that they just carry us away, and we end up in these long trains of associative thought and fantasy that we sometimes don't even notice for several minutes until we click, 'Oh right, I'm supposed to be meditating', and back we come.

The second of the four tasks is to let go of all that. To disentangle ourselves from these reactive fires. We're not trying to get rid of them or suppress them. They are, after all, entirely naturalistic processes, the legacy of our evolutionary past, that are simply part of what we are. It's not about trying to figure out a way in which they just don't happen any more, which would be nice, but highly unlikely. It's far more about the challenge of, 'Well, how do I deal with this stuff?'. I suspect all of us, as we've been here for nearly a week now, have become quite intimate with these reactive patterns. Yet what do we *do*? How *do* we work with them?

The Buddha's answer, and I think it's pretty much the answer we find in Sŏn as well, is that actually you don't do anything. You embrace this reactivity, this fear, this resentment, this attraction, this lust – whatever it might be – and you simply allow it the freedom and space to play itself out. If we don't identify with it, or reject it, or get caught up in it, it will follow its natural course as a transient, contingent phenomenon and fizzle out of its own accord.

Of course, that doesn't mean that it won't come back again – it will, and probably sooner rather than later – but the point is that this allows us a way of being with these reactions in which we have them, they don't have us. We begin to assume a responsibility, an authority, a stability, a clarity whereby we can begin to come to terms with these reactions so that they cease to be a power over which we seem to have very little control. But this is not achieved by doing something, it is achieved by just allowing ourselves to dwell in a non-reactive space, whereby these things are allowed to rise and pass away in full consciousness and awareness.

As this happens we might experience moments in which we suddenly realise that they have gone. We find ourselves in a still, clear, open space of awareness. This stopping of reactivity allows us to glimpse what it's like not to be caught up in those familiar patterns at all. These moments of stillness, of deep peace, are glimpses of nirvana itself: a state of presence that is not conditioned by the habits of reactivity. They may not last very long, but I think it's very important to consciously affirm and valorise them. And not just by making a mental note, but by exploring what it feels like in your body not to be reactive. Try and taste and enjoy the very flavour of this way of being.

In his *Straight talk on the true mind*, the Korean Sŏn patriarch Chinul confirms that nirvana is not some remote goal that we might reach one day if we're lucky but is at the heart of our life right now. For him, 'the sublime essence of nirvana is complete in everyone. There is no need to search elsewhere; since time immemorial, it has been innate in everyone.'[31] For the Buddha too, nirvana is 'clearly visible, immediate, inviting, uplifting, personally experienced by the wise'.[32] The third of the four tasks is to affirm this for oneself in one's own lived experience.

But these nirvanic moments are not the final goal of the practice. They are what allows us the freedom to be able to respond to the life that we're living – within ourselves, in relation to others, in response to social or political issues – from another perspective, one that is no longer driven by what we crave, what repels us, what we're confused about. Rather than letting ourselves be prompted to behave impulsively, blindly following whatever habit surges up in the moment, we discover a freedom that allows us to act in a way that is no longer conditioned by reactivity. Many of the *kongans* of Sŏn Buddhism illustrate such moments when a student is liberated from her or his reactive habits and suddenly utters something surprising in their own voice that is unconditioned by these things.

Unfortunately, like 'truth', this term 'unconditioned' is often placed on a metaphysical pedestal. Fortunately, though, you can easily spot this move by the unwarranted but telltale capital 'U': the 'Unconditioned'. For the Buddha, unconditioned (*asaṅkhata*) simply meant not to be conditioned by greed, hatred and confusion, i.e. reactivity. It is a synonym for nirvana. And like nirvana, it grants an ethical rather than a metaphysical freedom, the freedom to think and speak and act unconditioned by reactive patterns. What opens up here is what Buddhists call the noble eightfold path, which is comprised of how we see the world, how we make choices, how we speak, how we act, how we work, how we focus our energies, how we pay mindful attention, and how we become 'collected' and unified though samādhi.

This non-reactive space allows us to engage with life from a new perspective. It's like, in a way, being born anew into a life that's freed, to some degree at least, from these reactive habits and prompts. But what's all this got to do with the practice of Sŏn?

In Sŏn Buddhism, there's hardly any mention of the Four Noble Truths – let alone the way I've just rejigged them as four tasks. Yet central to Sŏn is the practice of taking what are called the four great vows. These vows are recited daily in Sŏn monasteries in China, Korea and Japan. So what are these four vows? I'll read them out:

> *Sentient beings are boundless; I vow to liberate them all.*
> *Defilements are inexhaustible; I vow to sever them all.*
> *Dharma gates are numberless; I vow to learn them all.*
> *The Buddha's way is unsurpassable; I vow to realise it.*

Some years ago my friend and colleague Gil Fronsdal,[33] who had trained in Zen before becoming a Vipassanā teacher, suggested that these vows might be a version of the Four Noble Truths. That struck me as a very compelling idea, which I've thought a lot about since. A few months ago, I mentioned this possible connection while I was giving a talk at the Dharma Field Zen Center in Minneapolis, and someone in the audience referred me to a passage in the *Bodhisattva jewel necklace sutra*, a Mahayana text found in the Chinese Buddhist canon, which explicitly states that the four vows are a way of expressing the Four Noble Truths.[34] I was reassured to find Gil's hypothesis confirmed by the tradition itself. It provides yet further justification for regarding the four truths as four tasks: in this case, as vows that commit you to engaging in a course of action.

So we can move from truths to tasks, and from tasks to vows. Once they become vows, these tasks become ethical commitments. My hunch is that what Deshan and other Sŏn masters are doing is not just debunking metaphysical claims for the fun of it, or uttering outrageous comments because that's what's expected of them. I think they're making very sincere, albeit dramatic, rejections of ideology and metaphysics in order to bring us back to the immediacy of what is demanded of us as ethical beings.

The important thing with this practice is not what you believe. It's not even about gaining deep insights through meditation into the nature of yourself or reality. What really matters is whether this practice makes a difference in how you live: how you think, how you speak, how you act, how you work. The Sŏn tradition is quite consistent here.

As I've already mentioned, what I enjoyed about training in a Sŏn monastery is that work is an integral part of the monastic life. The monks have broken with the early rule, which forbids them to till the fields and grow crops. There's something about this way of life that's very much hands on. So, in taking these four vows, the Sŏn practitioner transforms the Four Noble Truths into overt ethical commitments, into ways of living in and relating to the world.

Sentient beings are boundless; I vow to liberate them all.

This, to me, is a natural extension of the first task to 'fully know suffering' or to 'embrace life'. Suffering is not an abstract, disembodied condition. Living beings suffer, and living beings are boundless. Living beings – from the birds in the trees outside right up to us meditating primates in this room – suffer pain. We suffer things that we would rather didn't happen to us: we get sick, we grow old, we die, we don't get what we want and we get what we don't want.

If we empathise with other beings, then our response to their suffering will be a longing for them not to suffer. This is what underpins the vision of the bodhisattva – these four vows are basically shorthand for the bodhisattva vow. So when the practice of 'What is this?' extends beyond the question of our own life to ponder the lives of others, then it will lead us to feel more empathetic to their suffering. And that's the foundation for consciously committing oneself – whether as a public ritual of taking a vow or just a sincere personal longing – to do whatever one can so that living creatures do not suffer.

Yet built into the very language of these four vows is an acknowledgement of their impossibility. If living beings are boundless, which they seem to be, there's no way that I will be able to liberate them all – that's a pipe dream. What matters here is that if we really did experience the world in this way, we could not but long to assuage the suffering of others. It might be unrealistic that we'll ever achieve it, but it's an urge that becomes less and less possible to ignore. So this practice may start with simply paying more careful attention to our own existence – the tragic dimension of our lives, our own fleeting presence on earth – but as we expand the sphere of our attention, it leads unavoidably to a reconsideration of what matters in terms of how we act, how we respond to the plight of others.

Defilements are inexhaustible; I vow to sever them all.

Here you can easily see the parallel with the second task, which is to let go of craving or reactivity – what in the later traditions are often called defilements (in Sanskrit: *kleśa*). And again, these are inexhaustible. Whether we like it or not, they will keep on rearing their heads. Of course, some people may be more subject to powerful emotions such as anger and lust than others. And there may be periods in our lives when they are less pronounced – as we age, for example. Likewise, as a practitioner, by not identifying with and thereby fuelling them we may diminish their power over us to the point where they seem to fade away. But the fact remains that they are rooted in our limbic system as the legacy of our evolutionary past, so they're always going to be around to some extent. So we shouldn't get complacent. They'll keep rising up and surprising us.

Nonetheless, we vow to 'sever them all'. 'Sever' might sound a bit harsh, but it's really just a way of describing this process of letting go, of not getting caught up in them, and thereby disempowering them. Kusan Sunim used to compare the question 'What is this?' to a sword that cuts through destructive thoughts (*mangsang*). So each time some negative thought or fantasy, some anxiety or depressing idea arises in your mind, you can cut through it by asking: 'What is this?'. You turn it from something that threatens to overwhelm you into something to be questioned, to be curious about. In doing this you transform it. The Sŏn approach is to turn what seems to be a dull, brute fact into a question. What is this thing that's rising up within me? And that in itself is already the first step to its losing its power over you.

So we can see how embracing suffering might lead to the longing to liberate all sentient beings from dukkha, and how letting go of reactivity is comparable to severing defilements, but the third vow is less obvious.

Dharma gates are numberless; I vow to learn them all.

What on earth has that got to do with the third task of beholding the stopping of reactivity?

'Dharma gate' is an expression that is peculiarly Chinese. I'm not aware that there is an equivalent in Pali or Sanskrit. But just think for a moment about the metaphor of a gate. A gate is an empty space framed by two pillars and a top beam through which you are able to enter into another space: a room, a garden, a pathway, whatever it might be. But what are dharma gates? And in what sense are they numberless?

I take a dharma gate to be any situation in life that can become a doorway through which you can enter the eightfold path. And since there is no situation in life that cannot be transformed into an opportunity to enter this path, dharma gates are therefore numberless. For this transformation to be possible, however, we need to respond to the situations we encounter non-reactively. So for a life situation to be a dharma gate requires that we appreciate its emptiness, or, more accurately, how we are free to respond to it without greed, hatred, egoism and so forth. This absence of re-activity, as we've seen, is nirvana. Such a non-reactive space may not last very long, but it's a moment of freedom that allows us to think, speak and act differently. It is in this sense that it becomes, metaphorically, a dharma gate: one that allows us to respond to the situation in a conscious, careful, caring way, rather than just blindly being propelled in what we say and do by the first emotion or thought that flares up in our minds.

The Buddha way is unsurpassable; I vow to realise it.

This clearly refers to the noble eightfold path, the way of life that becomes possible once our response is no longer determined by our habitual, egotistic reactivity. What is very striking about the Buddha way, or the eightfold path, is that it encompasses every aspect of our humanity. It's not just about becoming the world's best meditator. True: meditation, mindfulness and collectedness are very much at the heart of it, but a beating heart is what animates a body, which thinks, speaks, acts and engages with other bodies. Everything about us needs to be engaged in this practice.

So once we let go of the idea that to be enlightened means to understand the nature of reality as it really is, or to gain some privileged mystical insight into truth with a capital 'T' – the way of thinking that Deshan and other Sŏn masters are trying to shake us free from – then we shift into a practice that is inextricably tied up with how we respond to life in each moment, which is the foundation for engaging with the world in an ethical way.

Friday morning

Waiting and listening

Stephen Batchelor

I have found it helpful over the years to think of this Sŏn practice as having both a dynamic and a passive aspect. This reflects the traditional Buddhist distinction between vipassanā, which means insight, and *śamatha*, which means quietness or calm. Buddhists tend to understand meditation as a process that seeks to integrate and balance these two dimensions. So far in these talks I've given a lot of attention to the vipassanā or dynamic aspect of the practice, namely, the enquiry 'What is this?'. To pose this question has a certain kind of charge to it, an *urgency*, which is very central to what the exercise is about. We seek to focus our energies into the singular question of our own lives.

But at the same time we're doing this in the context of a

meditation retreat. We're spending our time in silence, our eyes closed or half closed, sitting still on a cushion. We're pursuing this enquiry in a contemplative space. And that differentiates it from how similar questions would be asked, say, by existentialist philosophers in a café on the left bank of the Seine with a cup of strong coffee in one hand, a Gauloises cigarette drooping from their lower lip, engaged in feverish conversations with other anguished intellectuals.

The questioning itself is certainly not unique to Sŏn Buddhism. In addressing the core issue of what it means to exist as a human being, it is universal. It is the framework within which we explore it – one of silent, contemplative practice – that is different. So it's important to spend a fair bit of time on a Sŏn retreat just getting oneself into a more quiet, calm, embodied awareness. We can do that simply through resting our attention on the breath or doing whatever enables us to settle in a still, open awareness. Then, once the mind has quietened down, gently introduce the question in such a way that it does not disturb the surrounding calm.

I suspect that many of us have spent the last days trying to find an equilibrium between the stillness on the one hand and the dynamism or the energy of the enquiry on the other. In my own experience this practice really comes into its own when these two dimensions achieve moments of integration. So I can ask this question in a very intense way, but also in a way that is still, embodied and centred, no longer prone to rushing streams of chaotic ideas and thoughts and emotions.

In particular, we try to make this question come alive as a sensation of perplexity that is beyond any kind of intellectual curiosity. In fact, the words can disappear as soon as we enter into that felt sense of enquiry.

But we can also benefit from teasing out more explicitly the contemplative frame within which this enquiry takes place. I have already spoken of unknowing as the flip side of 'What is this?'. Such unknowing – this 'I don't know' – is also, in a sense, a coming to rest. We come to dwell in a still open space, acknowledging the fact that we don't really know who we are or what is going on. Giving up the insistence on having an opinion about everything and always being right can be a huge relief, letting us come to settle in a quiet, humble acceptance of our bewilderment.

Within that unknowing there are other facets of this still, silent context of our enquiry that are helpful to cultivate. One of these is *waiting*. This needs to be contrasted with *expecting*, which is similar in some respects but crucially different in others. In Old English the connection between these two ideas was more obvious: we used to talk of *waiting* as opposed to *awaiting* (a word we don't use much any more). But in German the link is clearly audible in the words *warten* and *erwarten*: to wait and to expect.

Expecting is a kind of waiting, except it is a waiting for something about which you already have a preconceived idea. And therein lies the problem, because if we have read or heard anything about Sŏn Buddhism, we'll have become aware of people who have had breakthroughs, sudden moments of enlightenment and so on, which, unfortunately, may have planted seeds in our mind like, 'Gosh, I hope that's going to happen to me too!', and so we conjure up a picture based on what we've read second-hand, and assume that this is what will happen when we practise Sŏn.

Now it's impossible to engage fully in any human activity without a sense that it's worthwhile and going to benefit us in some way. With meditation we hope, quite naturally and legitimately, that this practice will lead us to insight and understanding. That's just a given in human experience and we wouldn't even have come on this retreat unless we had had some confidence that it was going to be worth our while. If a friend had asked you, 'Why are you going on that retreat?', presumably you would have been able rationally to justify your decision. You'd say: 'I'm doing this retreat because...' and whatever followed the 'because' would have been what you hoped would happen while you were here.

This is entirely natural – it's not a problem *per se*. It only becomes problematic when the notion of whatever it is we're looking for overrides or interrupts the silent posing of a question in a state of unknowing where we are simply present to whatever the situation might throw up. This leads to what may feel like a rather uncomfortable conclusion, namely, that whatever we might hope for, there can be no guarantee at all that it will happen. Just because you may have sat 10,000 hours on a cushion does not entitle you to any kind of insight or enlightenment.

We have to be open to the fact that we may not achieve anything at all that corresponds to our preconceived idea of what the goal of the practice might be. We have to *let go* of all such expectations. And that's easier said than done. You may have had moments in your meditation where you become really still, focused and clear, everything seems to be going very well (whatever that means) and then suddenly a little voice pipes up and says, 'Hey – maybe I'm on the edge of a really profound experience. I feel that something amazing is about to happen!' So you start getting excited, with the result that all your stillness and clarity dissolve and you lapse back into your all too familiar and tiresome patterns of indulgent self-centred thinking.

So what can you do about it? How can you prevent this from happening? Well, one thing is to consciously valorise the experience of just waiting. Waiting without expecting. And to try and differentiate experientially between the two. I think over time this begins to dawn on us anyway. There's a certain point in any form of meditation where the practice becomes self-validating. In other words, we do it not because of some hypothetical goal we might attain one day but simply because doing it is sufficient in itself.

That just to sit, to be focused, to enquire, to be mindful, is already enough. We don't need to add anything else. Kusan Sunim used to warn us against 'adding legs to a snake'. A snake doesn't need legs. It gets around perfectly well without them.

Waiting is a deep acceptance of the moment as such. We reach a point where we're sitting, questioning, asking, 'What is this?', but without any interest in an answer. We realise that our longing for an answer undermines the authenticity of the questioning itself. Can we be satisfied just to rest in this questioning, this puzzlement, this perplexity, but in a deeply focused and embodied way? Waiting without any expectation. We're not waiting *for* something, we're just waiting. I've found that helpful – maybe you will too.

But going hand-in-hand with this waiting is also, I feel, a quality of listening. In general, I find listening to be a very valuable part of meditative awareness as such, no matter what form of practice we're doing. But here, rather than just listening more attentively to the rooks in the trees, the noises in the room, or the quiet hush of silence, I'd like to think of listening as a *metaphor* for meditation. It's helpful to notice that when we talk about meditation we tend, unconsciously, to describe what we're doing by drawing on metaphors of sensory experience.

I'll give you a simple example. Take the word vipassanā. The prefix vi- is an intensifier, while *passanā* comes from *passati* in Pali, which means to see, hence the common translation of vipassanā as insight. If you think about it, a lot of the instructions we are given in meditation assume the suitability – even the pre-eminence – of an ocular metaphor. For example, we're told to *watch* the breath. But of course we're not really *watching* the breath because we've got our eyes closed and, in any case, the breath is not something you can see. Or we're told to *look* into the mind. We're told to see what's happening in our experience. 'See', 'look at', 'watch' – all of these are things we do with our eyes. In other words, to pay attention to our inner experience, which has neither colour nor shape, is compared to what we do when we look at something, or watch something, or see something with our physical eyes.

Now, this is the language that you'll find throughout the Pali texts too. The Buddha uses the terms *dassati, passati* (to look, to see) all the time. I'm not suggesting that this metaphor has no role at all to play. But a key feature of Sŏn is to disrupt or question underlying assumptions that have become so much part of our language that we don't even notice them any more. So instead of watching or seeing, you sometimes find Sŏn teachers instructing you to listen or hear. Just think about this for a moment. What is the difference in your experience between looking at something and listening to something? And what does that difference *feel* like?

When you are asked to watch something carefully, what do you do? You tend to narrow the focus of your attention onto the object, thereby letting it stand out in the wider field of vision, in order that you can look at it more precisely. What you're looking at is invariably something outside of yourself, 'over there' somewhere. What often happens in meditation is that we fail to acknowledge the metaphoric nature of the visual language being used. Quite unconsciously, we adopt an inner stance or posture that mimics the act of seeing. You might feel, for example, that when you're meditating there's a bit of you, in the back of your head somewhere, that's peering in on your body and breath and mental states. You've created a distance between an observer looking in and an object being observed.

But if you think about listening or hearing it's often completely the other way round. Rather than narrowing your attention on a particular sound 'out there', you open yourself up to allow the sound to enter you. When you listen to a piece of music in your living room, for example, what do you tend to do? Very often you dim the lights or close your eyes, then raise the sound so that it envelops you. Then you relax and let yourself be completely receptive to the sounds that enter you from all around. So the internal posture you assume is not that of a detached observer looking out onto something, but rather a completely vulnerable and open attention that allows sounds to stream into you from every direction. Now that's a very different inner stance. Your physical posture might be the same, but your mental posture is the opposite to that of looking at something.

There's a passage in a late Chinese Buddhist Mahayana text called the *Śūraṅgama sūtra*, which is often cited in Sŏn literature. Here you find the Buddha asking the assembled audience of bodhisattvas, 'What is the most effective way to enter into the stream of meditation?'. As is the nature of these sutras, you then go through page upon page of wrong answers before you get to the fellow at the end of the line who, of course, has the right answer. In this case it turns out to be Avalokiteśvara, the bodhisattva of compassion, who says, 'My method consists in regulating the organ of hearing so as to quiet the mind for its entry into the stream of meditation leading to the state of *samādhi* and the attainment of enlightenment'.[35] Yes; the *organ of hearing*.

This appears to be one of the source texts in Sŏn for this approach to meditation. So when you ask yourself, 'What is this?', then after the question has been posed and you are left in the silence that follows the fading away of the words, just listen for a response. This is a waiting kind of listening. You're not expecting a particular answer. And the way you open yourself to the possibility of a response is through attending to what is arising in the moment in a similar way as you would attend to the global presence of sound with your ears. It's a kind of receptivity, an openness, an attunement. But it is a very different kind of attention compared to when you look at or watch something carefully with your eyes.

What's remarkable about this wide-open attention of listening is that you can be just as concentrated and focused as when you direct your consciousness onto a particular point.

In fact, for many people the experience of listening to music is often their way of becoming most concentrated and present. I find that listening to music often allows me to become deeply still within myself in a contemplative way. It's a kind of meditation. And as we learn to appreciate music, we notice how it becomes increasingly refined and rich, subtle and complex. It can be profoundly moving too.

The experience of music can also serve as an example of how we can attend more meditatively to the natural sounds that are around us all the time. The composer John Cage wrote a famous piece called 4'33" – pronounced 'Four thirty-three' – where a pianist comes onto a stage, sits down at a piano, but doesn't touch any of the keys for four minutes and thirty-three seconds. I have only heard a version of this played on a penny whistle, but the result must be much the same. Because you expect to hear music, you prime yourself to listen, but instead of hearing a piano being played, you find yourself acutely attentive to all the ambient sounds in the concert hall. You become aware of the music of the world, the polyphony of life itself. And after a while, you find yourself enjoying it as you might a piece of 'real' music. This, of course, is very similar to the kind of meditative listening we are talking about here.

Of all the bodhisattvas, why does the *Śūraṅgama sūtra* have Avalokiteśvara be the one who has the right answer to the Buddha's question about meditation? This suggests that the organ or hearing, or listening, is associated with compassion, which Avalokiteśvara personifies. The figure of Avalokiteśvara underwent a significant change in moving from India to China. The Sanskrit name literally means 'lord of the world', which is very patriarchal. In Tibetan it was translated as 'Chenrezig' or 'the one whose eyes look down', which is also patriarchal (and note also the introduction of 'eyes'). But when it was translated into Chinese, it became 'Guanyin', which means 'the one who observes sounds'. The sounds that the bodhisattva of compassion attends to are not just random noises but moans of pain, calls for help. In such listening and hearing we open ourselves to the suffering of life itself. It's like when we say to someone, 'I hear you', we are not just registering that they are speaking loudly and clearly enough, but that we feel for them, we empathise with their suffering, we care for their plight.

In coming to China, Avalokiteśvara did not just change his name. He changed sex; he became a woman. He transitioned, as we would say today. The figure of Guanyin as a woman in flowing robes, often seated on a lotus flower, is one of the most popular Buddhist images in China – rather like that of the Madonna in Catholicism. So what started out as a male figure gazing paternalistically down onto the suffering world turns into a female figure who is open to hearing the sounds or the cries of the world. This too reflects the shift in posture we have been talking about here, a shift from looking at to opening up, from seeing to hearing, from the eyes to the ears.

To think of listening in this way can help us better understand how to attend to what arises in response to the question 'What is this?'. In posing that question, allow yourself to be completely open to whatever you 'hear' in the pregnant silence that follows, without any hopes or expectations. Metaphorically, you're waiting to hear a response rather than expecting to find an answer. The point of Sŏn practice is not to look for an answer, or to see the nature of reality. Again, pay attention to the metaphors we use unthinkingly.

You might find it helpful on our last full day together just to explore what it feels like in your body to be open to this question in the same way that you would open yourself to a piece of music or listen with total attention to the polyphony of the birds and wind outside, the occasional plane that flies overhead, the patter of rain on the windows. Listen more carefully, and at the same time notice how that listening is not just an opening of the mind but an opening of the heart, a vital concern or care for the world, the source of what we call compassion or love, which brings us back into the world of relationships that we will be returning to tomorrow.

Friday evening

TALK

The path of compassion

Martine Batchelor

This evening I want to explore the place of compassion in Korean Sŏn. A question that comes up repeatedly concerns the Theravāda tradition, which has given rise to insight (or vipassanā) meditation. It prescribes the cultivation of four main qualities: lovingkindness, compassion, sympathetic joy and equanimity. For its part, the Tibetan tradition suggests exchanges of self and others, and it teaches various practices of that type. Yet in the Sŏn tradition you've just got the question, 'What is this?'

Where then do we find the practice of compassion? We can look at this in two ways. One way would be to look at it in terms of whether we cultivate something directly or indirectly, and I talked about that at the beginning. It's what I experienced when I was in

Korea: after one three-month retreat, I noticed I was more compassionate in daily life; I thought of others before myself. That's when I realised, 'This practice works!'. I might just be asking, 'What is this? What is this?' but it also has the effect of diminishing self-centredness, so we're going to be more present for others.

The Korean Sŏn tradition strongly promotes a whole ethical training in compassion, though it occurs outside the sitting practice itself. As Stephen mentioned this morning, the tradition emphasises the three great trainings of ethics, meditation and wisdom. Whatever way you practise meditation, teachers in the tradition will tell you that it's not enough. If you just practice ethics, they'll say it's not enough. The same goes for wisdom. In order to develop on the path from the point of view of the Sŏn tradition, you need to cultivate these three aspects together: ethics, meditation, wisdom.

The tradition highlights what it calls the *Brahmajāla sutta* which, from the end of the first part, differs from the version of this sutta in the Pali canon.[36] The Korean version of this text is so important for Sŏn, I gather, because it contains the bodhisattva precepts. Every two weeks we'd recite it in the monastery, so I translated it in order to know what it was telling us to do. I could then understand why my fellow monastics carried out certain actions. And why Master Kusan did what he did. Because the bodhisattva precepts prescribe it.

I was enthralled by the effect that the Bodhisattva precepts had on the behaviour of the monks and the nuns, amongst themselves and with the lay people. Korean Sŏn nurtures an especially communal way of life, so the way you relate to each other is very important. You're not all tucked away in little private huts at all. You sit, sleep and eat in a room like this meditation hall we're sitting in now. It's your dining room, meditation room, changing room – you do everything there. Twenty to thirty people will be living together in this way, so they need to have a way to live together which inspires them to cohabit in harmony.

I suspect that the first part of the *Brahmajāla sutta* in the Pali canon was the source text. Then many other texts arrived in China and were translated. Around the fifth century CE, perhaps in 440, the bodhisattva precepts were incorporated into the sutta. To inspire adherents the text claims to come from the Buddha himself, but in reality much of it draws on Chinese culture. For instance, it mentions filial piety a lot, and this is very much a Chinese concept. Strikingly, the text laid down an ethics which fitted the time and culture, thus making it applicable to monks, nuns and laypeople. The nuns and monks recite the precepts every two weeks, and the lay people take them and renew them every year. This ethics avoids perfectionism. Rather, rests on the idea that we try as best we can to follow the precepts, knowing that adverse conditions might prevent us from getting it quite right. So we need to take the vows again every year to remind ourselves that ethics is an important part of the practice.

In this spirit I want to introduce you to the text in question tonight. It plays a vital part even now in helping us understand how we could live as dharma practitioners. In this way it is every bit as important as sitting in questioning meditation. First let me read to you a wonderful analogy from the text:

> *The ethical precepts are like a brilliant lamp which can disperse the darkness of the night.*

Cultivating ethics, cultivating relationships, thus acts like a bright light in the dark – a way of discerning what really matters in the way we live.

> *They are like a most precious mirror which is able to reflect the dharma in its entirety.*

We often come across a strong notion of awakening in Chan/Sŏn/Zen Buddhism, one that presents it as unconditional – 'going beyond ethics'. Sometimes you hear this strange term 'crazy wisdom', as if the precepts don't apply to awakened individuals. This key text refutes that idea. In terms of the practice, the precepts contain the whole dharma. The precepts apply to everyone. Finally:

> *They are like a most valuable gem which frees one from poverty and endows one with wealth.*

Modern culture often presents ethics as something re-strictive and claustrophobic – not *fun*. But here we find the sutta telling us that ethics gives us wealth, makes us rich, helps you to flower. Stephen talks about 'flourishing'; I see ethics as helping us to flourish.

So what are the precepts about, really? We have the ten ma-jor precepts and the 48 secondary precepts. Don't worry – we're not going to ponder each of them! Not all of them address situations we confront today. Bear in mind that the sutta in question emerged in the fifth century CE and expresses the local and cultural exigencies of that time and place. It's also a religious text born of competition with other religions and other traditions – a feature I've noticed in every text I've translated. Even in the Sixth Patriarch's *Platform sutra*, a seminal text for the Sŏn tradition, a third of the text ad-dresses competition with other traditions or sects. Another third deals with historical and geographic matters. The remaining third actually speaks to our times – an extraordinary achievement given its remoteness in time.

Each precept has a succinct statement, followed by a little explanation, The first precept establishes the pattern:

> *Refrain from taking life.*

But that's not all there is to it.

A disciple of the Buddha must refrain from taking life either by performing the act of killing himself, by causing someone else to do it, by doing it in a roundabout way, by praising death, ...

It doesn't just say, 'Don't do this,' as in 'Do not cause harm'. Rather, it's setting out various ways in which we can cause harm. We might not cause harm directly, but we can do so indirectly, as well as cause someone else to cause harm on our behalf! In this way the precept addresses the conditionality of ethics. It goes on to make this link explicit:

One must never intentionally kill a living creature by creating the cause or conditions for death, or by developing a means of taking life, ...

Our intention to harm is important here. We could cause death accidentally, which would make a big difference. Unless you keep causing accidents, of course – in which case we need to inquire into our intention and what conditions it. A bodhisattva (or sincere practitioner) aspires to awakening. She or he must always be compassionate. Compassion is the nub of the precept. It explores the various conditions which help or hinder our acting compassionately.

The next precept reads:

Refrain from taking what is not given.

The explanation that comes after it follows the same pattern: refrain from the unskilful action yourself, don't cause somebody else to commit it, and so on. Again, the explanation asks us to look at conditions impinging on our behaviour, at the way we actually behave, the way we relate to others, at the circumstances. At bottom, it is addressing causes and conditions.

Thirdly:

Refrain from harmful sexual behaviour.

This precept doesn't condemn sexual activity, but counsels against sexual behaviour that causes harm. Is our sexual expression causing harm to ourselves, to others – even in a roundabout way? Then you have:

Refrain from telling lies.

Fourthly (and I love this part):

She or he must never convey the impression that they saw something that they didn't see, or didn't see something that they did see. Either by physical gesture or by mental intention.

This is getting subtle: we mustn't convey the wrong impression when we speak. And even if we don't say anything, we can deliberately convey the wrong impression by physical gesture, or even remaining silent when we know what the other person assumes something that we know to be false. The mental intention to deceive or manipulate remains effective. I find this subtlety beautiful. They prompt us to ask, 'How do I speak? What do I say? Is it true?'.

I had a friend who decided that, for three months, she wasn't going to talk to other people about someone who wasn't present. She said her conversations diminished radically as long as she followed the rule. Following the precept launches an inquiry into relationship to speech, to honesty, and to truth.

Fifth:

Refrain from praising yourself and slandering others.

Basically don't praise yourself and put others down so that you can elevate yourself even further, thus don't create the causes and conditions, etc, and this is a duty of the bodhisattva. And here comes possibly the most difficult thing that's being asked of us:

The bodhisattva takes upon her- or himself the slander directed towards others, transfers whatever is unpleasant to herself, and credits others with whatever is good.

Are we prepared to do that? Sometimes I feel we're not even prepared to consider it, but it's salutary to think about its implications of 'taking upon oneself the slander directed towards others'. I had a friend who took on this precept. He worked at a recovery centre, and sometimes one of his colleagues would say 'Well, X did this!' Whereupon my friend would say, 'Oh no, no, I did it, I did it, I did it!'. So then the others present would exclaim, 'You did it?'. That changed the tenor of the whole incident.

Are we prepared to take the blame for what is unpleasant like my friend did? That is really, really tricky. We have a negative bias whereby we're quick to notice even a little unpleasantness, whereas we're slower to notice even significant positive experiences. This bias can colour our relationship to the world. We want everybody to be safe and happy, but not if it takes something from us. Nevertheless, that's what's often asked of us: can we extend ourselves and be a little less comfortable so as to give whatever is good to others? When we ourselves are well endowed, can we share what we have with others? This conduct would reinforce our appreciative joy, altruistic joy.

Then comes the sixth precept:

Refrain from reviling others in order to spare yourself.

This rules out putting somebody down to avoid giving them something or helping them. 'Oh! They're really bad, you know! No, no! I don't have to help them.'

Seventh precept:

Refrain from being angry, and when someone comes to ask forgiveness, treat that person well.

Here we're given two aspects to consider. One aspect is wonderful, I really like this one:

A bodhisattva should be kind to others and not quarrel. She or he should present a compassionate state of mind. If, on the contrary, a bodhisattva should abuse a living creature or vent their anger on an inanimate object...

In those days they might have kicked the cart, I presume. Nowadays we might kick the computer, or the tyre of a car. I love the sheer humanity of this precept; it implicitly asks us to watch what happens when we get angry? Usually wisdom flies out the window at that point. The precept isn't suggesting that anger is bad *per se*, it's saying when we're angry we're likely to do something stupid, even destructive, and certainly something we'll regret afterwards.

The text takes up a particular form of stupidity if we hold onto our anger: we don't forgive another person when s/he asks us to. This is a really serious transgression. In itself forgiveness is a fascinating issue. We have a tendency to forgive, but we don't forget. So we might say, 'Yes, I forgive you'; but a few months later we might remind the other person of their trespass against us. To me that's not true forgiveness.

In the monastery in Korea I marvelled at how the precept was observed. People readily asked for forgiveness, and it was just as readily granted. If you made a mistake, the only thing you needed to do was to go to someone – usually someone a little higher up in the hierarchy – bow three times, and say, 'I made a mistake'. That was it! It was forgotten, never mentioned again. We westerners had difficulty with this procedure. If Master Kusan told one of us that we'd made a mistake, we'd present excuses and explanations. I could just see the Koreans thinking, 'Gosh, all they need to do is bow three times, and that'd be the end of it'.

I was struck by the beauty of this tradition of forgiveness. Just saying, 'Yes, I made a mistake' opened the door to understanding how we made the mistake, recognising it, and then letting somebody know that we recognised it. And the other person would answer something like, 'Okay, yeah, you did that. Hopefully you've learned from this and you won't do it again.'

Now we're getting down to the minor precepts:

> *Care well for those who are sick. As a disciple of the Buddha,*
> *upon seeing someone who is afflicted with a disease, you must*
> *care and provide for her or him as you would care for the*
> *Buddha himself.*

So: care for those who are sick when you encounter them; see them as if they were the Buddha himself being ill, and take great care. Show them great compassion, great respect. The Pali canon contains an account of an episode in the Buddha's own life in which he highlights the need to care for the sick. The Buddha and his companion visit a community of monks, and they find one of them lying helplessly ill on the ground, covered in his own excrement. The two visitors immediately wash him, bring him inside and put him to bed.

Understandably the Buddha then demands an explanation of the other monks' neglect. 'Well, he was ill, and of no use to us in his condition. So we saw no point in looking after him,' came the reply. The Buddha's response was mild under the circumstances. He reminded the monks that they had no father or mother with them, no one else to take care of them – they needed to take care of each other. Then he delivered the punch line: 'Whoever would serve me should serve the sick.' So compassion isn't something to be marketed or traded. We have to see each person as valuable in their own right. Korean Sŏn trains us to ask: 'Can I see each person as the Buddha himself, as a bodhisattva?'.

Then come some very practical precepts. I love the precision of some of these texts. They seem to arise from quite specific situations. For example:

> *Don't beg for and try to obtain things by relying upon the authorities. A disciple of the Buddha must not extort money or goods or seek any other kind of gains by relying on the power of a king, a prince, a minister of state, or government official with whom they are closely acquainted.*

This, I suspect, is about influence and corruption. It's saying: try to avoid being corrupt, try to avoid using other people's authority. Then you have:

> *Save the lives of living creatures and set loose those who are about to be killed.*

This precept ushered in the ritual of saving living creatures on certain auspicious days. Thus began the strange custom whereby people sell live animals to Buddhists who buy them in order to release them. The sellers then catch them again to resell to other Buddhists. This custom survives to this day. I read in a travel book from the 1800s, that big monasteries were like zoos – they harboured animals that were too old to work in the fields, but could live out the rest of their lives in these monasteries. The latter maintained enclosures for the animals, which the monastics fed from the donations of lay supporters. So the precept isn't just an idea – it becomes something practical; something that arises out of causes and conditions, and creates other causes and conditions.

Again:

Refrain from anger. Do not strike others. Do not take revenge. A disciple of the Buddha must not repay anger with anger, or blows with blows.

This is so difficult to do, isn't it? If somebody is angry with you it's so hard not to answer in kind. And does it help? This is the important question: does it work?

In France, we have a preoccupation with tombs, ones situated in village cemeteries. A whole family in the village might have a family tomb that can accommodate up to eight coffins. A problem arises as more family members die and the tomb approaches capacity.

One day, after a funeral of a member of another branch of my maternal family, a relative told my mother and me that our family couldn't use the tomb any more because we'd used up our quota, and we weren't as directly related anyway. My mother was upset because she wanted to be interred there, along with my father, my brother, and her own mother. So I offered to try to negotiate a solution.

I phoned a member of the other family I knew quite well. As we talked our voices started to become louder and louder. She'd say something, and I'd say, 'Wait a minute!', and advance my own claim; then she'd retort, 'Wait a minute!', and do likewise. It was becoming unpleasant. I realised that this wasn't helping. So then I took another tack: I dropped my tone of voice; I used softer words. She followed suit. In this way we found a solution. The interaction demonstrated the value of the questions implicit in the precept: does anger work? Is there another way?

At a deeper level this precept asks: can we creatively engage? When we meet anger, can we creatively engage with it? The first question it poses is whether the problem is about me, or is it about the other person? Did I do something out of place, or not? If yes, how can I creatively engage with that? If I didn't do anything inappropriate, then the other person has to own the problem themselves. But how can I stay stable and open?

That's where meditation comes in. We need to get a sense of the three trainings building upon each other. Ethics underpins meditation, which develops wisdom, which deepens ethics, then meditation clarifies ethics. The causal arrows can go in the opposite direction as well. All three of the trainings are important and nourish each other.

Here comes another very practical precept:

Do not ply an unwholesome, harmful occupation.

A disciple of the Buddha must not, with harmful intention and for the sake of gain, engage in such occupations as selling physical charms or men or women... (It goes on to stipulate other items that ought not be traded.)

Then comes other, quite different injunctions (ones coined before the rise of psychoanalysis, of course!) against:

interpreting dreams, predicting the sex of a child, making use of spells or magic, performing tricks in order to deceive others, preparing any kind of dangerous drugs, and concocting poisons out of gold, silver or the venom of insects.

In different times and places the list will change. Our own time and culture have thrown up other unwholesome occupations that harm others directly, or favour my own interest at the expense of others'. Nowadays we might be hard put to it to identify an occupation which is totally unharmful. We have to bring wisdom to bear on this conundrum. Some cases are fairly obvious, though. I had a friend long ago who was looking for work in Australia. At the time, the only job he could get was in a factory where he had to kill chickens. After a day, he said, 'No way, I can't do this!'.

Then you have:

Pay a ransom and rescue people from their difficulties.

Another precept I want to bring up succinctly goes like this:

Do not cause harm to sentient beings.

A disciple of the Buddha must not sell swords, clubs or bows or arrows, nor should they use uneven balances or inaccurate weights and measures.

But here's another curly one:

One must not use one's influence with government office

to deprive others. You should not deprive others of their possessions, have others bound and shackled, or undo the achievement of others.

What might bodhisattva precepts appropriate to our own time look like? Could each of us create a list like that? Or, as a community, how could we put such a list together, in light of the causes and conditions that we encounter now? I have a lot of friends who are involved in 'engaged Buddhism'; they're reflecting on this very question and creating an ethics for our time.

In January, Stephen and I went on a pilgrimage to Sri Lanka, where we met Dr Ariyaratne, the founder of the Sarvodaya movement. He was one the first modern engaged Buddhists in the late 1950s and early 1960s. He wanted to help villagers to help themselves, but though he was a Buddhist himself, he wanted to be open to and support any villagers, regardless of their religion. He didn't help just Buddhist villages, given that Sri Lanka comprises Buddhist, Hindu, Muslim and Christian communities.

This meeting was very inspiring. I already knew about Sarvodaya, but hadn't realised how his project embraced all communities at a time when the government did very little for villagers. He found it hard to get the government to pay attention to what he was doing, which had its upside in that he could help people, and help them to help themselves, independently and creatively with a small organisation. This amazing movement continues to this day, and has diversified. It also tried to foster peaceful dialogue when war broke out between Sinhalese Buddhists and the Tamil Hindus and Roman Catholics.

These precepts in the *Brahmajāla sutta* help us to see that yes, meditation is a great boon, but we also have to work on our relationships, how we use resources, how we relate to others, and how we engage in politics. When we talking about ethics, we're also touching on politics. A key precept says: *Do not join a war camp*. Do not be an envoy with harmful intentions. It finds application in many aspects of our collective existence. We must never lose sight of ways in which we can bring our compassionate ethics to bear, even in small ways.

What is this? *Ancient questions for modern minds*

Saturday morning

FAREWELL

Practice in daily life

Stephen Batchelor

So, our retreat is coming to an end. Most of you must have packed, vacated your room and are getting ready to go home. Just take a moment to reflect on how you feel as part of this group now as compared to when you arrived. Strangers have become familiar, even though you may have exchanged no more than a few words with them over a bowl of porridge this morning. We've only been here a week, but something has happened: we have slowly become a community of sorts. You may already feel disappointed that tomorrow you will no longer see the person who has been sitting next to you, behind whom you have been walking round this room all week. Or that man whose name you still don't know but with whom you have come to enjoy cutting vegetables together in the kitchen every morning.

I like to think of the end of the retreat as the beginning of the real practice.

Notwithstanding occasional hiccups, it is relatively easy to meditate when you have nothing else to do, all your basic needs are met, you're cut off from contact with family, friends and colleagues, you hardly speak to anyone, and every day follows the same unvarying schedule. But remember that all this has been a training for what you will be returning to this afternoon. If you can only practise Sŏn under such highly controlled conditions, then frankly it will not be of much use – unless, of course, you want to spend the rest of your days in a hermitage.

I have a friend called Josh who spent several years as a Zen monk in the United States. At a certain point, Josh decided he had had enough of formal training and the time had come to apply what he had learned in the outside world. So he left the monastery, rented an apartment on Sixth Avenue in New York, and embarked on a career in public relations. Above the door that led from his living room to the street, he put up a sign that read 'Zendo' (meditation hall). Instead of going to a monastery to practise, Josh turned this notion on its head and learned to practise on the sidewalks and in the offices of the metropolis.

Imagine something similar here, a sign that says 'meditation hall' above the centre's front door that opens to the courtyard outside and the roads, villages and towns beyond. Think of every single situation in your life as an opportunity for practice. Don't hanker nostalgically for Gaia House as that one place where you can quieten your mind and think clearly. Don't get me wrong: I'm not discounting the value of retreats. All I'm saying is that we should think of a retreat as a means to an end rather than an end in itself. A retreat from the everyday is not done in order to devalue the everyday by adopting a more 'spiritual' way of life. It is done so you can return to your daily life renewed and refreshed, with a sharper moral focus and a clearer sense of what really matters for you.

I also think it helpful to expand what we mean by 'practice', a word that is bandied around nowadays but often with little reflection. If you were to line up a bunch of Buddhists and ask them to name their practice, I suspect many of them would refer to a particular spiritual exercise: 'I practise Zen', 'I practise Vipassanā', 'I practise Dzogchen', and so on. But this alone is a very narrow understanding of practice.

The word the Buddha used that perhaps comes closest to our word practice is, in Pali and Sanskrit, *bhāvanā*. Bhāvanā means to 'cultivate' or 'develop' something – literally to 'bring something into being'. So we could also translate it as to 'create'. And what is it we cultivate, develop or create? The path itself, a way of life that encompasses all of our humanity. For the Buddha, every aspect of the eightfold path was to be bhāvanā-ed, or practised: the way we see ourselves and the world, the way we form intentions and ideas, the way we speak to each other, the way we act, the way we make our living, the way we apply ourselves – and, only then, the way we pay mindful attention and focus our minds in meditation. Practice involves far, far more than just meditating.

Instead of practising meditation can we learn how to practise being human? This is what the Greeks called 'self-governance'. This starts with a conscious decision to leave behind a life of thoughtless habit and reactivity and embark on a life of self-creation, in which we work towards becoming the kind of person we aspire to be. And we can extend this further into striving to create the kind of world we aspire to live in as well. This is what it means to live ethically. Ethics is not just about observing precepts. It has to do with actively creating the kind of person we want to become and the sort of society we would like our children to live in. In this sense, the eightfold path is ethical through and through.

There's no reason at all why your practice could not be what you do for your livelihood rather than the kind of meditation exercise you do once or twice a day. Yet since most Buddhist traditions have been centred around monastic institutions and come to regard the wise and kind renunciant as the ideal dharma practitioner, they have privileged competence in meditation and expertise in doctrine (i.e. what monks are supposed to spend their time doing) as the central elements of what it means to practise. I think this is a distortion and bias that we no longer need. I'd go further: this privileging of monasticism sets up an unhealthy hierarchy, where 'lay' people are expected to defer to monks on pretty much everything, thereby tacitly reinforcing the monastic model of dharma practice as the ideal. I know many monks and nuns. They are all sincere, intelligent and well-intentioned people, who might even agree with much of what I'm saying. But the institutions they represent embody a system that preserves an authoritarian, paternalistic power structure based on inflexible orthodoxies that the individual monastic can do little to modify or change.

Another way of looking at this would be to acknowledge that meditation does indeed lie at the centre of one's practice, but in the same way as a hub functions as the centre of a wheel. The value of the hub lies in its connecting the spokes to the rim and tyre, thereby enabling the wheel to operate as a wheel. In isolation the hub is just a useless piece of metal. Similarly, if your meditation is not integrated into the rest of your life, it too could serve little purpose beyond developing a certain stillness and clarity of mind. This might provide a degree of inner wellbeing yet fail to animate the kind life in which you flourish fully as a person in all aspects of your humanity.

When you get home and go back to whatever you do, you will have plenty of opportunities to expand your practice into your thinking, speaking, acting and working. You will notice how rapidly and insistently the events of life bombard you, leaving little if any time to ponder on how to respond to their pressures and demands.

You will not have the luxury of retreating to Gaia House for a few days to meditate on what you should say or do. Your response is demanded immediately. You have to risk saying or doing something that in hindsight you might come to regret. But you have no choice. This is how we learn to refine our moral compass: by acting and then carefully attending to how the consequences of our actions play out – both in ourselves and on others. Of course we will sometimes get it wrong. The world is simply too complex and fast moving to be able to understand every subtle nuance of a given situation. And no matter how much meditation we do, we will never be able to know in advance what the effects of our actions will be.

Some of you might discover how alone you can be in this kind of practice. On a group retreat like this we are surrounded by others of like mind, but when you get back to Stoke-on-Trent you might find that most people you meet don't look at life in this way at all. There are a number of things you can do to reduce this sense of isolation in your practice. Make a point of developing friendships with people who share your deepest values and interests. Attend local meditation and study groups, and don't worry too much if their approach is not identical to your own. Seek out places like churches to spend time in quiet contemplation. Join online discussion groups and virtual internet communities. Read widely – not just books on Sŏn, but anything that inspires you to practise, no matter what tradition it comes from. Listen to dharma talks from audio archives. And explore what the arts have to offer: in literature, film, theatre, poetry, painting, dance, sculpture. There is such a wealth of material available in all these fields.

Above all, remember that your life is a work-in-progress, an unfinished project, and your practice is whatever drives this process forward. Be courageous, take risks, and don't mind failure.

As Samuel Beckett put it: 'All before. Nothing else ever. Ever tried. Ever failed. No matter. Try again. Fail again. Fail better.'[37]

 Notes

1 Born near Shanghai, Sheng-yen (1930–2009) was a monk, scholar and one of the foremost Chan teachers in Taiwan in the 20th century. He taught widely in the United States and Europe.

2 For an authoritative account of the life and work of Chinul (1158–1210), see Buswell (1983, 1991).

3 Cited in Batchelor (2015b), p. 29. Mazu Daoyi (709–788) was a student of Nanyue Huairang. Huairang was the monk who was instructed by the Sixth Patriarch Huineng to ask the question: 'What is this?'. On Mazu and his teachings, see Ferguson (2000), pp. 65–71.

4 Ferguson (2000), p. 68.

5 James (1890), p. 301.

6 Urgyen Tulku Rinpoche (1920–1996). Regarded as one of the most renowned teachers of Dzogchen of his time, he was the father of Chökyi Nyima, Tsoknyi, and Mingyur Rinpoche, all of whom have become prominent Dzogchen teachers with centres around the world.

7 Saṃyutta nikāya 35.23. Bodhi (2000), p. 1140.

8 Yamada (2004), p. 11.

9 Yamada (2004), case 38.

10 Yamada (2004), case 18.

11 I have been unable to trace the source for this citation.

12 Majjhima nikāya 10. Ñāṇamoli and Bodhi (1995), pp. 145–6.

13 Lucretius (2007). Book II, lines 1030–9.

14 Sengai Gibon (1750–1837) was a Japanese artist-monk of the Rinzai school of Zen best known for his *sumi-e* brush paintings.

15 S.N. Goenka (1924–2013) was a highly influential Indian/Burmese vipassanā teacher who established a worldwide network of meditation centres. Stephen attended retreats with Goenka in India in the early 1970s.

16 Heidegger (1978), p. 317.

17 A student of Shitou and Mazu, Layman Pang (740–808) is the best known lay Chan teacher of his time. For this kongan, see Cleary and Cleary (1977), p. 301, and Ferguson (2000), pp. 95–6.

18 Richard J. Davidson (b. 1951) is the William James and Vilas Research Professor of Psychology and Psychiatry, Director of the Waisman Laboratory

for Brain Imaging and Behavior, and Founder of the Center for Healthy Minds at the Waisman Center, University of Wisconsin-Madison. Davidson has been one of the key figures in the conferences and dialogues on science and Buddhism organised by the Mind and Life Institute under the Dalai Lama.

19 Cited in Holmes (1998), p. 130.

20 See Batchelor (2015a), chapter 9.

21 Gittings (1966), p. 41.

22 Cited in Motion (1997), p. 227.

23 Gittings (1966), p. 87.

24 Seung Sahn Sunim (1927–2004) was the founder of the worldwide Kwan Um school of Zen.

25 For a fuller account of this episode see Batchelor (2017) pp. 17–19.

26 Kassaka sutta: The farmer (SN 4.19).

27 Dahui Zonggao (1089–1163) He was the dominant figure of the Linji school during the Song dynasty. Dahui introduced the practice of kan huatou, or 'inspecting the critical phrase', of a kōan story. This method was called the 'Chan of gongan (kōan) introspection' (Kanhua Chan). Although he believed that kōans were the best way to achieve awakening, he also recognised the teaching of Confucius and Laozi as valuable.

28 On Deshan Xuanjian (819–914) and his teachings see Ferguson (2000), pp. 196–200. This passage is cited on p. 199.

29 Ferguson (2000), p. 198.

30 From the poem 'Preludes' (1917). See Eliot (1963), p. 25.

31 Buswell (1983), p. 162.

32 *Anguttara nikāya* III:55. Bodhi (2012), p. 253.

33 Gil Fronsdal (b. 1954) is an American Buddhist teacher. Ordained as a Sōtō Zen priest in 1982, he received dharma transmission in 1995. He currently teaches in the vipassanā tradition at Insight Meditation Center and Sati Center for Buddhist Studies, which he established in Redwood City, California, as well as Insight Retreat Center in Santa Cruz.

34 As a source, the person referred me to Shohaku Okamura's *Living by vow*, pp. 15–16, and the footnote on p. 258, which provides the reference to the bodhisattva in Jewel necklace sutra in Taisho vol. 24, p. 1013. According to tradition, this sutra was translated into Chinese from Sanskrit between 376 and 378 CE. Recent research suggests that it was in fact composed in China sometime in the fifth or sixth centuries. The four vows seem to have been used in the Tiantai school of Buddhism prior to being adopted in Chan.

35 Lu K'uan Yü (1966), p. 142.

36 DN 1 Brahmajāla sutta: The all-embracing net of views.

37 Cited in Knowlson (1996), p. 674. This line became the inspiration for Beckett's novella *Worstward ho* (1983).

References

Batchelor, Martine (2005) Women in Korean Zen. Syracuse: Syracuse University Press.

Batchelor, Martine (2010a) The path of compassion: the bodhisattva precepts. New Haven & London: Yale University Press.

Batchelor, Martine (2010b) The spirit of the Buddha. New Haven & London: Yale University Press.

Batchelor, Stephen (2015a) After Buddhism: rethinking the dharma for a secular age. New Haven & London: Yale University Press.

Batchelor, Stephen ([1990] 2015b) The faith to doubt: glimpses of Buddhist uncertainty. Berkeley: Counterpoint Press.

Batchelor, Stephen (2017) Secular Buddhism: imagining the dharma in an uncertain world. New Haven & London: Yale University Press.

Bodhi, Bhikkhu, tr. (2000) The connected discourses of the Buddha: a new translation of the Saṃyutta nikāya. Somerville: Wisdom Publications.

Bodhi, Bhikkhu, tr. (2012) The numerical discourses of the Buddha: a translation of the Aṅguttara nikāya. Somerville: Wisdom Publications.

Burke, Edmund ([1757] 1998) A philosophical inquiry into the origin of our ideas of the sublime and beautiful. London: Penguin.

Buswell, Robert (1983) The Korean approach to Zen: the collected works of Chinul. Honolulu: University of Hawaii Press.

Buswell, Robert (1991) Tracing back the radiance: Chinul's Korean way of Zen. Honolulu: University of Hawaii Press.

Cleary, Thomas, and JC Cleary, tr. (1977) The blue cliff record. Boulder: Shambhala Publications.

Eliot, TS (1963) Collected poems 1909–1962. London: Faber & Faber.

Ferguson, Andy (2000) Zen's Chinese heritage: the masters and their teachings. Boston: Wisdom Publications.

Gittings, Robert, ed. (1966) Selected poems and letters of John Keats. London: Heineman.

Heidegger, Martin (1978) Basic writings. David Farrell Krell ed. London: Routledge, Kegan & Paul.

Holmes, Richard (2008) The age of wonder: how the Romantic generation discovered the beauty and terror of science. London: HarperPress.

Holmes, Richard (1998) Coleridge: darker reflections. London: HarperCollins.

James, William (1890) The principles of psychology. New York: Dover Publications.

Kierkegaard, Søren ([1844] 1957) The concept of dread. Walter Lowrie tr. Princeton: Princeton University Press.

Knowlson, James (1996) Damned to fame: the life of Samuel Beckett. London: Bloomsbury.

Kusan Sunim ([1985] 2009) The way of Korean Zen. Martine Batchelor tr. Boston: Weatherhill/Shambhala.

Lucretius (2007) On the nature of things. AE Stallings tr. London: Penguin Classics.

Lu K'uan Yü (Charles Luk) tr. (1966) The Śūraṅgama sūtra. London: Rider.

Motion, Andrew (1997) Keats. London: Faber.

Ñāṇamoli, Bhikkhu, and Bhikkhu Bodhi, tr. (1995) The middle length discourses of the Buddha: a new translation of the Majjhima nikāya. Boston: Wisdom Publications.

Okamura, Shohaku (2012) Living by vow. Somerville: Wisdom Publications.

Yamada, Kōun, tr. (2004) The gateless gate: the classic book of Zen koans. Somerville: Wisdom Publications.

About Gaia House

In 1983, with the support of a community of meditators, Christina Feldman and Christopher Titmuss founded Gaia House in an old vicarage in the village of Denbury, Devon. The name 'Gaia' was chosen for two reasons: Gaia was the name of the Greek mother earth goddess, now seen as a symbol for the interrelationship and interdependence of all things sharing this planet, and it echoed 'Gaya', the name of the city in northern India near where Gotama attained awakening.

Gaia House became a Trust with registered charitable status in 1990. Due to the steady growth of interest in insight meditation, in 1996 the Gaia House Trust bought the former manor house and Christian nunnery of West Ogwell, where it is currently located.

Today, Gaia House is one of the largest residential meditation centres in Europe. About 1,500 people from all backgrounds and walks of life attend group and personal retreats there each year, practising meditation in an atmosphere of silence. They are supported by a residential team of eight volunteer coordinators and a permanent team of paid staff. The nine members of the teacher council as well as other invited teachers offer a comprehensive range of retreats year round. To support their ongoing practice and create community, meditators have formed sitting groups around the United Kingdom affiliated to Gaia House.

The peace and beauty of Gaia House provides a sanctuary of calm stillness, welcoming all people who wish to explore the heart of understanding and freedom. Retreat fees are kept as low as possible, so that all who wish to attend are able to do so.

In addition to retreat fees, Gaia House relies on donations to keep its doors open, and will continue to depend on people's generosity to ensure it continues into the future as a comfortable and hospitable place able to offer refuge and inspiration.

To make a donation, please visit the Gaia House website. Your support is much appreciated.

Gaia House Trust is a registered charity, No. 900339.
www.gaiahouse.co.uk • **info@gaiahouse.co.uk** • phone **+44 1626 333613**

FINDING MEANING IN A DIFFICULT WORLD

The Tuwhiri Project was set up in 2018 with the intention of helping people find meaning in a difficult world by producing educational resources for secular dharma practitioners and communities.

As well as publishing books with a focus on early Buddhism, its retrieval, and secular adaptation to twenty-first century conditions, we are creating online courses that will help people develop a secular take on the dharma.

Tuwhiri is the initiative of secular dharma practitioners in Australia and Aotearoa New Zealand. *After Buddhism: a workbook* was our first book, *What is this?* our second, and others are on their way. A word in te reo Maori, tuwhiri means to disclose, reveal, divulge, make known, or a clue, a means of discovering or disclosing something lost or hidden, a hint, a tip, a pointer.

The Tuwhiri Project Ltd is owned by Aotearoa Buddhist Education Trust (ABET), a New Zealand registered charity. As a social enterprise with no investor shareholders and so no need to prioritise profit-making, we can focus on our purpose – to help people find meaning in a difficult world.

We are immensely grateful to all the Tuwhiri Sponsors, Book Supporters and Kickstarter backers who helped breathe life into the aspiration that has become Tuwhiri, and for the time, energy and expertise so generously given to this project by people, communities and organisations around the world.

To continue to produce books and develop online courses, we need your help. In Aotearoa New Zealand, you can make a charitable donation through ABET for The Tuwhiri Project to 38-9019-0064662-07. Wherever you are in the world, you can donate using a debit card or credit card by going to:

https://www.tuwhiri.nz/donate

After Buddhism: a workbook

Each time the teachings of the Buddha entered a new culture outside their Indian birthplace, they have had to undergo renewal and reinterpretation so as to gain traction in the new host society.

Stephen Batchelor's work represents a landmark in Buddhism's sinking roots in the modern west, and his *After Buddhism* is his most systematic contribution to the process. What is being left behind, he suggests, by the 'after' in the title is a set of received, conventional misrepresentations of the teachings, not their true beating heart.

After Buddhism: a workbook is the consummate guide to this thought-provoking work. It provides a basis for periodic group and individual study of Batchelor's text. Winton Higgins's humorous, easy-to-read text offers a fresh and accessible commentary on *After Buddhism* without compromising the depth of Batchelor's experience, scholarship and ideas.

Jim Champion's astute questions encourage readers to use Batchelor's reissue of the Buddha's teachings to reflect more deeply on the lives they're leading, the individuals they're becoming, and the world we inhabit.

Use this workbook to run a course for your sangha, or to deepen your own understanding of *After Buddhism*.

"Winton Higgins's series of talks on Stephen Batchelor's After Buddhism provided our group with deeper insight and clarity around this modern, secular take on the Buddha's message."
— Dr Izak Janowski, Golden Wattle Sangha

Published 2018, 140pp

Individual copies can be bought in paperback, Kindle, PDF and ePub formats through our online store: https://www.tuwhiri.nz/store. Small quantities of the paperback for course use can be purchased at a special low rate.

The book is also available through local bookshops as well as Amazon, Book Depository and elsewhere.

CPSIA information can be obtained
at www.ICGtesting.com
Printed in the USA
LVHW081025240220
647985LV00005B/77